MARKETING LAW

Joe L. Welch

MARKETING LAW

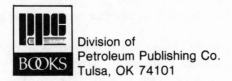

Division of
Petroleum Publishing Co.
Tulsa, OK 74101

Library of Congress Catalog Card Number: 80-80645
International Standard Book Number: 0-87814-107-3
Printed in the United States of America

1   2   3   4   5   83   81   80   79

A special thanks to these people
for their influence and support:

My wife, Lydia

Alfred Cox
Rowe Meador
Jack Starling

CONTENTS

PREFACE

Accompanying the public demand for more socially responsible business has been a proliferation of statutes and public policy statements which significantly influence marketing decision-making. As the laws become even more pervasive and agencies continue to assume a more dominant position, demands on marketers to understand the scope and importance of these issues will expand. This book provides managers and students with necessary information to incorporate these important legal and public policy contingencies into marketing plans and strategies.

Marketing Law is written in understandable terms for the student and practitioner. All marketing and legal concepts are defined so that legal and marketing prerequisites will not be necessary. Also, *Marketing Law* can appropriately be used in undergraduate and graduate public policy, consumer policy, and marketing management courses.

The book is organized to facilitate examination of the various laws which affect each aspect of the marketing mix: distribution, pricing, product, and promotion. Chapter 1 provides an overview of the legal issues, a historical examination of antitrust and consumer legislation, and an introduction into the practices of regulatory agencies. Chapter 2 deals with legal issues which effect interchannel and intrachannel decision-making. Chapters 3 and 4 identify and examine the various laws and court decisions which constrain pricing decisions. Specifically, there is an in-depth examination of price fixing and price discrimination. Chapter 5 explores all recent legal developments in promotion. In addition to discussing deception and the basis for evaluating deception, the chapter examines advertising to children, comparison advertising, advertising of professional services, and FTC remedies. Chapter 6 examines laws which impact on such product-related decisions as packaging, labeling, warranties, product safety, and trademarks. Finally, Chapter 7 identifies existing and proposed laws which are consistent with the "consumer right to know" mandate of the Federal Government.

Following each chapter is a set of discussion questions which requires assessing various aspects of marketing law. Answering these questions will provide additional insight into the strengths and weaknesses of public policy.

I am genuinely indebted to the many people who contributed to the success of this book. I specifically acknowledge the following people for their contributions: Dr. Alfred Cox for initially stimulating my interest in antitrust and consumer law; Dr. Louis E. Boone for his insightful comments and advice as the book developed; Estelle Doyle for her efficient typing assistance; Kathryne Evans Pile for her invaluable editorial comments; and my wife, Lydia, for her ideas, patience, and support.

Joe L. Welch

1 MARKETING LAW: AN OVERVIEW

Marketing is a complex system of business activities designed to plan, promote, and distribute want-satisfying goods and services to potential consumers. Being a multifaceted activity, marketing involves internal policy and strategy development and requires significant interaction and policy development among distribution channel members such as other manufacturers, agent and wholesale middlemen, retailers, and ultimate users. Furthermore, the marketer must be sensitive to consumer needs, social objectives, governmental policies and demands, and competitive rights and obligations as suggested by the principles of free enterprise.

Some of the primary objectives marketers strive to achieve by implementing product, price, promotion, and distribution strategies are (1) expansion of identified markets; (2) penetration of existing markets; (3) maintenance of constant growth; (4) expansion of market share; (5) achievement of profit and return on objectives; and, in some cases, (6) maintenance of the status quo. Abundant historical evidence indicates that specific marketing policies which are developed to achieve these organizational objectives are often not consistent with such rules of free enterprise as maintenance of competition, free price, and freedom of market entry. For example, some industrial organizations have determined that there is a direct relationship between market share of a product and the product's profitability. This implies that early in a product's life cycle, companies should develop strategy which has as its primary objective the rapid development of market share. One way to accomplish such an objective, of course, is to acquire competitors' products and, therefore, the customers that normally purchase the acquired brands. Because of the subsequent market dominance achieved by the acquiring firm, significant barriers to entry into that market could also develop. This case of product acquisition to achieve market dominance illustrates a relatively common example of conflicting objectives—i.e., market share and profit vs. barriers to entry and lessening of competition.

1

In addition to contradicting the rules of free enterprise, some marketers' practices are in conflict with the rules of social responsibility such as "the consumer's right to know," a philosophy which was established by the consumer and recently mandated by the government. For example, companies have long recognized that consumers believe there is a relationship between package size and price per unit (i.e., quantity discount when buying larger packages). By utilizing this relatively common consumer perception as the basis for strategy development, companies could easily deceive by (1) marketing an excessively large number of package sizes which would make unit price comparisons virtually impossible and (2) pricing larger packages at a higher unit price than smaller packages. The result is consumer deception. The consumer purchases the larger package to get a price break but, unknowingly, is actually paying a higher unit price.

Although most anticompetitive and deceptive activities are practiced by only a small percentage of companies, they do exist and do jeopardize the rights of consumers as well as the rights of companies that compete within the framework of free enterprise. In order to strengthen the competitive process and preserve the rights of consumers, the government has designed statutes which help prevent anticompetitive and deceptive business practices. This chapter will present an overview of the various regulatory statutes as well as introduce the reader to agencies which have been commissioned to enforce these laws. Specific marketing activities and the legality of such activities will be detailed in subsequent chapters.

Significant Legislative Enactments

1890—Sherman Antitrust Act. Outlawed monopolies as well as contracts, combinations, and conspiracies that restrain trade.

1914—Clayton Act. Regulated price discrimination, tying contracts, exclusive dealing arrangements, requirements contracts, reciprocal deals, and acquisition of stock of another company.
AMENDMENTS TO CLAYTON ACT:
1936—*Robinson-Patman Act.* Regulated seller induced price discrimination, buyer induced price discrimination, and price discounts (i.e., advertising allowances, brokers' discounts).
1950—*Celler-Kefauver Amendment.* Regulated acquisition of assets as well as stock of another company.
1976—*Hart-Scott-Rodino Antitrust Improvement Act.* Required large firms to pre-notify FTC of intentions to merge.

1914 — Federal Trade Commission Act. Declared unfair methods of competition to be illegal; established the Federal Trade Commission.

AMENDMENTS TO FTC ACT:

1938 — *Wheeler-Lea Act.* Prohibited deceptive acts and practices as well as unfair methods of competition.

1973 — *Alaska Pipeline Act.* Increased penalty for violating a cease and desist order; allowed injunctive relief.

1975 — *FTC Improvement Act.* Expanded idea of trade regulation rules; expanded remedial powers of FTC.

1966 — Fair Packaging and Labeling Act. Prevented deceptive packaging and labeling practices; facilitates price comparisons.

1968 — Consumer Credit Protection Act. Required full disclosure of credit terms. Included Truth in Lending Act, Equal Credit Opportunity Act, Fair Credit Billing Act, Fair Credit Reporting Act, Fair Debt Collection Practices Act, and Consumer Leasing Act.

1972 — Consumer Product Safety Act. Regulated activities related to product safety; adopted safety standards for products; banned hazardous products; recalled defective products; and established Consumer Product Safety Commission.

AMENDMENTS TO CPSA

1976 — *Consumer Product Safety Commission Improvements Act.* Consumers can sue Consumer Product Safety Commission; expanded authority of CPSC.

1975 — Magnuson-Moss Warranty Act. Required disclosure of warranty terms in easily-understood language.

Antitrust Movement — An Introduction

Early development of the United States' economic system was characterized by small, geographically-dispersed organizations serving relatively small, local markets. With the development of faster, and more efficient transportation and communication systems, however, non-local markets became more accessible and the newly-developed organization form — corporation — took advantage of these new opportunities. Not only did corporations pursue new markets, but they also began integrating horizontally and vertically in order to realize the recently identified benefits of economies of scale and to take advantage of a tax break which was available to vertically integrated firms. This process of accumulating power through internal and external expansion continued throughout the nineteenth century until most economic and political power was controlled by an alarmingly small number of individuals.

Accumulation of power was also facilitated by prevailing social doctrine of the 1800's. Specifically, *laissez faire* ideology of the 1700's suggested that business be controlled only by market forces and that survival be realized by the economically fittest. The best way to accomplish this goal of survival was to expand, eliminate competitive pressures, and optimize production processes. Therefore, companies engaged in some of the following activities: (1) development of trusts and holding companies and the subsequent monopolization of entire industries; (2) organization of pools to divide markets without competing; (3) rebates to secure customers; (4) discrimination in price to favored customers; and (5) horizontal and vertical price fixing arrangements. Widespread practice of such abuses placed free enterprise in serious jeopardy of not surviving.

During the latter part of the nineteenth century, people began to understand the dangers of monopolies and conspiracies to eliminate competition. The first attack on monopolies was directed at railroads and resulted in passage of the Interstate Commerce Act of 1887 which (1) outlawed practices of railroads to divide markets, fix prices, and discriminate in price, and (2) established the Interstate Commerce Commission as the regulatory agency.

Subsequently, the same farm groups, labor groups, and small businessmen that were instrumental in effecting passage of the Interstate Commerce Act obtained support from the Federal Government to eliminate other monopolies that endangered free enterprise. In 1890, Benjamin Harrison signed into law the Sherman Antitrust Act, which eventually became one of the most significant weapons for attacking counter-competitive business activities.

Sherman Act

The Sherman Act required that businesses act independently rather than in concert with competing businesses. The act's proponents wanted to maintain free competition by eliminating unfair accumulations of power. This was generally accomplished by prohibiting (1) "Every contract, combination, or conspiracy, in restraint of trade or commerce among the several states, or with foreign nations" (Section 1) and (2) "Monopolies or attempts to monopolize" (Section 2).

Although the Sherman Act was initially interpreted by the courts to mean literally that all restraints of trade were illegal, it was subsequently interpreted in 1911 to refer only to restraints which are "unreasonably restrictive of competition." With the adoption of this *rule of reason* concept, it was the court's role to interpret the reasonableness of restraints in order to ascertain their legality.

In addition to restraints which require *rule of reason* interpretation, there are certain restraints which the court considers to be *per se* violations of the Sherman Act. Once the court has had sufficient experience with a particular business practice to make a summary judgment that the practice has no positive competitive characteristics, it may declare the practice to be illegal *per se*. Practices which are *per se* violations of the Sherman Act include vertical and horizontal price fixing, horizontal division of markets, and tie-in arrangements.

Within two decades after passage of the Sherman Antitrust Act, it became evident that the law had some major deficiencies in preventing certain practices. First, the Sherman Act lacked specific definition of the legality of business practices. Second, unreasonable restraints had to exist before the Sherman Act could be applied. As was witnessed in the early 1900's, once monopolies were developed it was difficult to reverse their negative effects on the character of the competitive environment. For example, the steel industry was relatively fragmented in the 1800's until U.S. Steel acquired most of the independent producers and therefore controlled over 60 percent of steel output. Similar to the steel industry, most of the nation's other oligopolies were also formed by uncontrolled merging immediately after passage of the Sherman Act.

Clayton Act

In order to give the courts more specific guidelines with regard to various marketing practices and to stop anticompetitive restraints of trade in their incipiency, the Clayton Act was passed by Congress in 1914. With the Sherman Act, practices were legal unless the government could specifically identify that competition had been adversely affected. With the Clayton Act, however, practices could be declared illegal if they had the probable effect of substantially lessening competition or creating a monopoly.

Specifically, the Clayton Act prohibited the following practices "where the effect of the practice may be to substantially lessen competition or tend to create a monopoly in any line of commerce."

(1) Price discrimination—Section 2

(2) Exclusive agreements (including tying contracts, reciprocal arrangements, and requirements contracts)—Section 3

(3) Acquisition of stock of other companies (merging)—Section 7.

Robinson-Patman Amendment

The Clayton Act remained unchanged until the 1930's, which brought the depression and the rapid rise of supermarket chain stores. Since these giant food stores purchased in relatively large quantities, they could command significant power and therefore influence sellers into offering them special prices and services which were not made available to smaller, independent food stores. The result of these discriminatory practices was to place independent grocers at a competitive disadvantage. In order to restrict discriminatory practices between sellers and large-scale buyers, Congress passed one of the nation's most controversial and complex antitrust laws, the Robinson-Patman Act. As an amendment to Section 2 of the Clayton Act, the Robinson-Patman Act imposed the following prohibitions.

Section 2(a) states that it is illegal to discriminate in price between purchasers of commodities of like grade and quality where the effect of the discrimination may be to lessen competition substantially or to create a monopoly. Section 2(a) also indicates that the seller can justify a price differential if (1) it costs the seller less to transact with a particular buyer or (2) the price change is based on changes in market conditions or deterioration of merchandise.

Section 2(b) states that a seller may offer a price differential if it is made in good faith to meet the equally low price of a competitor.

Section 2(c) states that brokerage discounts can only be given to third party brokers who are independent of both the buyer and seller.

Sections 2(d) and (e) state that services, facilities, and promotional allowances cannot be offered to a buyer unless the assistance is offered to all competing buyers on proportionally equal terms.

Section 2(f) states that it is unlawful for a person to induce as well as receive a discrimination in price.

Antimerger Amendment

In 1950, Section 7 of the Clayton Act was amended by the Celler-Kefauver Act to prohibit acquisition of assets as well as the stock of another company when the effect of the acquisition is to lessen competition substantially or to create a monopoly. Prior to passage of this amendment, only acquisition of stock was illegal. The Celler-Kefauver Amendment plugged this loophole in the law.

Merger Prenotification

Section 7 of the Clayton Act was also amended in 1976 with passage of the "prenotification section" of the Hart-Scott-Rodino Antitrust Improvement Act. Generally, the Act requires that all large firms notify the Federal Trade Commission of merger plans prior to final consummation of the acquisition. In addition to merger prenotification, the law also amended the civil antitrust procedures by (1) giving the Attorney General the power to secure information which may be important to an antitrust case from a third party, and (2) giving any State Attorney General the right to bring suit for citizens of the state (i.e., *parens patriae*, class action suit) against companies that violate the Sherman Act.

Federal Trade Commission Act

As a reaction to development of trusts, inadequacies of the Sherman Act, and demands by businesses to be protected from anticompetitive activities of other businesses, President Wilson re-emphasized to Congress the need for unambiguous antitrust policy legislation (1914). After considerable disagreement and debate between the Congressmen, it became evident that specific definition of illegal business activities was futile; numerous exceptions to any definition and new, unidentified illicit activities would undoubtedly appear after passage of such a law. Congress, therefore, agreed on a flexible law which (1) declared unfair methods of competition to be illegal (Section 5) and (2) established the Federal Trade Commission (FTC) as an investigative and regulatory agency. The FTC's primary role is to protect businesses and consumers from business activities which are unfair, deceptive, or anticompetitive. Because of the general nature of the FTC Act, the commission now has the flexibility to investigate numerous business activities such as advertising, preticketing, lotteries, pricing practices, and distribution activities.

FTC as a Consumer Agency

In order to expand the FTC jurisdiction and authority, the Wheeler-Lea Act was passed in 1938 as an amendment to the Federal Trade Commission Act. The FTC Act became, for the first time, a consumer-oriented law, and the Federal Trade Commission took on the characteristics of a consumer agency. Specifically, the Wheeler-Lea Amendment added to Section 5 the prohibition of deceptive acts and practices as well as unfair methods of competition. In addition, the FTC was (1) given power to initiate investigation against companies without waiting for formal complaints; (2) given the right to regulate acts and practices which deceive consumers (and not just businesses); (3) given authority to issue cease and desist orders; and (4) given power to fine companies for not complying with cease and desist orders. Finally, the new FTC Act required companies to appeal cease and desist orders within 60 days.

Along with giving the FTC additional rulemaking and regulatory power, the consumer orientation was again strengthened in 1975 with passage of the Federal Trade Commission Improvement Act,[1] and in 1973 with the Alaska Pipeline Act. The FTC Improvement Act provided the following:

(1) Expanded the idea of trade regulation rules and gave the FTC the right to define specific practices which are unfair or deceptive.

(2) Allowed the FTC to fund the participation of consumer groups and other interest groups in rulemaking proceedings.

(3) Permitted the imposition of fines for violating trade rules.

(4) Declared that finalized cease and desist orders can serve as the basis for penalizing other companies that subsequently engage in the practice even if they were never given a cease and desist order.

(5) Stated the FTC can get restitution for deceived consumers by changing deceptive companies' contracts, forcing companies to refund money, forcing companies to pay damages, or forcing companies to make public notification of the deceptive acts.

The Alaska Pipeline Act increased the penalty for violation of a cease and desist order from $5,000 to $10,000 and gave the FTC the authority to obtain injunctions against unfair or deceptive acts or practices.[2]

Federal Trade Commission

As indicated in Figure 1-1, the FTC is directed by 5 commissioners who are appointed by the President of the United States for a term of 7 years. One commissioner is designated by the President as chairman and is given managerial responsibilities for the FTC's operations. Other staff members of the FTC, such as the Director of Public Information, Executive Director,

---

[1] Gerald G. Udell and Philip J. Fischer, "The FTC Improvement Act," *Journal of Marketing,* 41 (April 1977), pp. 81-85.

[2] J. Halverson, "The Federal Trade Commission's Injunctive Powers Under the Alaska Pipeline Amendment: An Analysis," *Northwestern University Law Review,* Vol. 69, No. 6 (1975).

and Chief Administrative Law Judge, are appointed by the chairman and confirmed by the commissioners.

Major activities of each FTC department are listed on the organizational chart (Figure 1-1).[3]

Figure 1

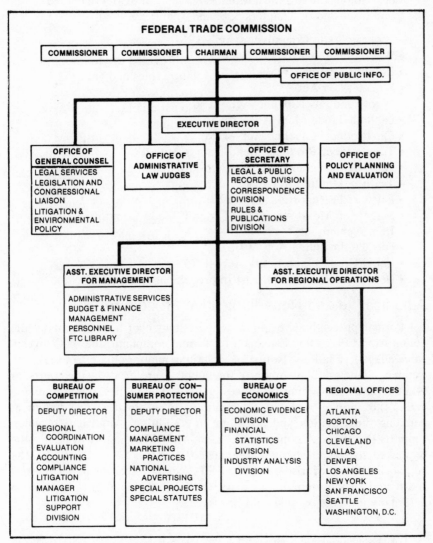

[3]"Your Federal Trade Commission, What It Is And What It Does," *Federal Trade Commission*, U. S. Government Printing Office, 1977.

Laws Regulated

The FTC has extremely broad authority to regulate numerous activities of American business. It controls unfair competitive practices of business and also is a consumer protection agency. Specifically, it has been given authority to regulate credit, labeling, packaging, warranty, and advertising practices. Among the specific laws and associated activities regulated by the FTC, and discussed in Chapters 5, 6, and 7, are:

- Federal Trade Commission Act—1914
- Webb-Pomerene Export Trade Act—1918
- Robinson-Patman Act—1936
- Wheeler-Lea Act—1938
- Wool Products Labeling Act—1940
- Lanham Trade Mark Act—1946
- Fur Products Labeling Act—1951
- Textile Fiber Products Identification Act—1958
- Fair Packaging and Labeling Act—1966
- Truth in Lending Act—1969
- Fair Credit Reporting Act—1970
- Magnuson-Moss Warranty—Federal Trade Commission Improvement Act—1975
- Fair Credit Billing Act—1975
- Equal Credit Opportunity Act—1975
- Hart-Scott-Rodino Antitrust Improvement Act—1976

Adjudicative and Nonadjudicative Procedure

Formal proceedings begin with the issuance of a complaint by the commission.[4] Preceding issuance of a formal complaint, the FTC investigates alleged violations. Notice of violations may originate from (1) government agencies, (2) members of the public, (3) referrals by the courts, or (4) Federal Trade Commission investigations. The request for commission action (i.e., notice of violation) should be an informal, signed statement detailing the violation and providing any additional information which supports the claim. A commission "examiner" subsequently evaluates the request to determine whether interstate commerce is involved, whether the activity is under the jurisdiction of the FTC, and whether the public interest is affected. If these conditions exist, the FTC begins an investigation to determine if a complaint should be issued.

---

[4]For more information see: "Organization, Procedures, Rules of Practice, and Standards of Conduct," *Federal Trade Commission*. Also, "The Federal Trade Commission: Modes of Administration," *Harvard Law Review*, Vol. 80 (March 1967), pp. 1063-1108.

During the investigation but prior to issuance of the formal complaint, the commission may dispose of the case by accepting a *consent order* or obtaining *voluntary compliance.* The consent order waives the rights of both parties to further procedural steps and details the manner in which the business will comply. After the consent order is submitted to the commission for consideration, it is placed on public record for 60 days during which time the commission will receive and consider public views concerning the order. If the consent is subsequently rejected, a complaint is issued and the adjudicative process begins. If the consent order is accepted, the business is bound to the conditions of the order just as if it were a formal, adjudicative decree. If, on the other hand, the law is being violated but the public is safeguarded, the commission may informally dispose of the case by obtaining *voluntary compliance* from the business. Voluntary compliance does not have the same effect as an adjudicative order.

If the case cannot be handled through nonadjudicative procedure (i.e., consent order or voluntary compliance), the Federal Trade Commission will issue a complaint and litigate the case before an FTC Administrative Law Judge or a Commissioner who is serving as a Law Judge. The Administrative Law Judge's initial decision must be made within 90 days after completion of the presentation of evidence, and either party may then appeal the decision to the commissioners within 30 days.

If a decision of the Administrative Law Judge is appealed, the commissioners may review and rule on the case by issuing a cease and desist order or dismissing the charges. If a cease and desist order is issued, the business has 60 days to appeal the decision to the U.S. Court of Appeals. On the other hand, if charges are dismissed, no appeal can be made by the FTC.

Penalties

In order to deter unfair and deceptive business activity and obtain remuneration for injured consumers, the FTC has been given the following remedial powers:

1. Imposition of fines
2. Recision or reformation of contracts
3. Refund of money or return of property
4. Payment of damages
5. Public notification of the rule violation or the unfair practice.

Prior to passage of the Magnuson-Moss Warranty—FTC Improvement Act in 1975, *fines* could only be imposed on persons, partnerships, and corporations that actually violated a cease and desist order. Company A, therefore, could engage in an unfair or deceptive act or practice and realize the profits from such an activity without being fined. Also, Company B could practice the same deceptive activity as Company A, even after

Company A received a cease and desist order, and not be subject to a fine. This illustrates one of the primary problems with the pre-1975 FTC law: imposition of fines for anticompetitive or deceptive activity was not applicable until after a cease and desist order was issued and then the fines could only be applied to the company receiving the order.

In 1975, the FTC's authority relative to fines changed. The FTC can now impose a $10,000 fine per violation on companies or persons that violate (1) a cease and desist order previously given to the offender; (2) a cease and desist order given to any other firm in the industry; or (3) a trade regulation rule (discussed in the next section). In other words, a cease and desist order given to one firm is applicable to all firms in the industry even if they are not subject to the order.[5] Also, each day of noncompliance to the order represents a separate violation and, therefore, a $10,000 fine.[6] Firms must, therefore, carefully monitor legal developments in their respective industries and take steps to avoid violating cease and desist orders given to other companies.

The FTC also has authority to rescind or reform a company's contracts in order to rectify injury to consumers or companies resulting from deceptive or unfair activities or violation of FTC rules. For example, in 1976 the FTC initiated action against Borden, requiring them to develop a contract to license their ReaLemon trademark to "any competitor willing to pay a royalty of one-half of 1 percent of net sales."[7] According to the FTC, Borden had gained monopolistic power by utilizing predatory and discriminatory pricing.

Although the FTC does not have authority to impose punitive damages on violators of the law, they can force companies to refund money which was obtained through deceptive or unfair acts or practices. They can also require violators to pay damages to injured consumers or companies as well as force them to notify the public of the wrongdoing. For example, Warner-Lambert was required to state in future advertisements that "Listerine will not help prevent colds or sore throats or lessen their severity."[8] The corrective message had to be placed in all Listerine advertisements until $10 million had been spent. The action was taken by the FTC because Warner-Lambert had falsely represented that Listerine would cure or

---

[5]For a discussion of the implications of this law, see: Gerald G. Udell and Philip J. Fischer, "The FTC Improvement Act," *Journal of Marketing,* Vol. 41, No. 2 (April 1977), pp. 83-84.

[6]The fine was increased from $5,000 to $10,000 by passage of the Alaska Pipeline Act in 1973. For more discussion, see: Dorothy Cohen, "Remedies for Consumer Protection: Prevention, Restitution, or Punishment," *Journal of Marketing,* Vol. 39, No. 4 (October 1975), pp. 28-29.

[7]"In Re-Borden's ReaLemon Trademark," *Journal of Marketing,* Vol. 40, No. 4 (October 1976), p. 121.

[8]"High Court Rejects Warner Lambert Bid to Review Order to Correct Listerine Ads." *Wall Street Journal,* April 4, 1978

prevent colds. Since many people envisioned Listerine as a cold preventative, the corrective message was necessary to change consumers' perception of the mouth wash.

Trade Regulation Rules

Trade regulation rules are designed to expedite the process of issuing cease and desist orders for activities which are clearly deceptive or unfair. Although the FTC has been developing the rules since 1962, the Court and Congress did not confirm their rulemaking authority until the early 1970's. Upon confirmation of this authority, the FTC developed the following types of rules: (1) interpretive rules—general statements of policy which only interpret the FTC's views with respect to unfair or deceptive acts or practices; (2) substantive rules—specifically defined acts or practices which are unfair or deceptive. Although the commission does not have recourse against violations of interpretive rules, it can utilize all available penalties to obtain restitution for violation of substantive rules.

In order to develop a substantive rule, the FTC must publish notice of the proposed rulemaking activity in the Federal Register and state the reason for the rule. They must then allow interested parties to submit written arguments and views for public examination. Subsequently, the commission conducts informal hearings in order to give interested parties the opportunity to present their positions. The Magnuson-Moss Warranty—FTC Improvement Act allows the commission to fund the participation of (1) interested groups, (2) persons who have ideas which are vital for fair determination of the rulemaking proceedings taken as a whole, and (3) a person who cannot afford to pay costs of participation. Also, Congress provided the commission $1 million per year to utilize as compensation for these qualified, interested parties. However, not more than 25 percent of the fund can be used to compensate persons who would be regulated by the proposed rule.

Consumer Protection Statutes

Because of business' insensitivity to the needs of consumers and their exploitation of consumers, Congress enacted a series of laws designed to protect consumers. The first of these laws—the Food, Drug, and Cosmetic Act—was passed in 1906 and amended in 1938 to protect consumers from the adulteration of food and the misbranding of food, drugs, cosmetics, and therapeutic devices. Also, during the 1930's companies found it profitable to substitute an inexpensive product for an expensive product without notifying consumers of the switch. Some of the affected products included wool, fur, and textiles. To protect consumers by requiring accurate identification of such products, Congress enacted the Wool Products Labeling Act, Fur Products Labeling Act, and Textile Fiber Products Identification Act in 1939, 1951, and 1958, respectively.

Although Congress partially remedied several problems with passage of the labeling laws, the Food, Drug, and Cosmetics Act, and the FTC Act, there were still numerous activities that had not received adequate attention from legislators. In the 1960's and 1970's, however, many consumer inequities were identified and resolved through a Congressional "consumer right to know/consumer protection" mandate. Following is a summary of the laws which make up this significant development in marketing law (extensive discussion of each law is presented in Chapters 6 and 7):

• *Fair Packaging and Labeling* (1966) — prevented deceptive labeling of consumer products and facilitated price comparisons.

• *Truth in Lending Act* (1968) — required creditors to disclose credit terms and cost of credit conspicuously so that consumers could make informed decisions.

• *Fair Credit Reporting Act* (1971) — gave consumers the right to inspect credit reports and to correct mistakes made on such reports.

• *Consumer Product Safety Act* (1972) — monitored and regulated matters related to product safety; established safety rules; banned and recalled products; gave jurisdiction to administer the Flammable Fabrics Act, Federal Hazardous Substances Act, Poison Prevention Packaging Act, and Refrigerator Safety Act.

• *Fair Credit Billing Act* (1975) — helped credit customers correct mistakes made on their billing statements.

• *Magnuson-Moss Warranty Act* (1975) — required disclosure of warranty terms in easily-understood language.

• *Equal Credit Opportunity Act* (1975) — prohibited discrimination in any aspect of the credit transaction because of sex, marital status, race, national origin, religion, age, or receipt of public assistance.

• *Consumer Product Safety Commission Improvement Act* (1976) — expanded power of Consumer Product Safety Commission; permitted consumers to file civil suit against CPSC.

• *Fair Debt Collection Practice Act* (1978) — made it illegal to harass or abuse any person and make false statements or use unfair methods when collecting a debt.

Department of Justice—Antitrust Division

Organized to investigate and regulate the development of monopolies and other business conspiracies that restrain trade, the Antitrust Division of the Department of Justice has sole responsibility for investigating and prosecuting companies which violate the Sherman Act and joint responsibility with the Federal Trade Commission for monitoring activities delineated in the Clayton Act. As indicated in Figure 2, the Antitrust Division is managed by an Assistant Attorney General who reports to an Associate Attorney General. The division is organized to provide primary emphasis on policy planning, enforcement and litigation, and economic policy development. The objectives have recently been facilitated by development of the economic policy department, the special trial section, and the policy planning and legislative office. The division has also become more active in investigating activities which are injurious to consumers through its consumer affairs section.

Investigation and Litigation

Investigation of business conduct begins when a business, the public, another government agency, or the division's own staff issues a complaint which indicates that a particular business or industry is engaging in unlawful practices. Upon receipt of a complaint, the Antitrust Division normally notifies the Federal Trade Commission of its intention to investigate a particular activity. Interaction between the two agencies is necessary to insure that the agencies do not waste time and money by overlapping their investigations.

Formal investigations may be carried out by the division's own field staff or, when in-depth research and interviewing are necessary, by the Federal Bureau of Investigation. The division may also rely on a secret Grand Jury investigation. The Grand Jury subpoenas information that must be copied and presented to the court by the companies under investigation. Utilization of the Grand Jury is common because it expedites the data collection procedure and provides for severe penalties for noncompliance. Subsequent enforcement of antitrust statutes takes place in the District Court. Decisions of the District Court can be appealed by either party to the Court of Appeals and the Supreme Court.

During the investigative process, the Assistant Attorney General in charge of the Antitrust Division must decide whether or not to take criminal or civil action against a possible offender. Although the division is primarily interested in criminal violations, it will pursue civil action when changes need to be made in the character of a particular company or industry or when it cannot be established that the company willfully violated the law. In other words, criminal action is taken in order to punish the offender for willfully violating the law.[10] The court can fine or imprison the violator for

---

[9]Price fixing is the most common criminal case prosecuted by the division.

Anitrust Division
Figure 2

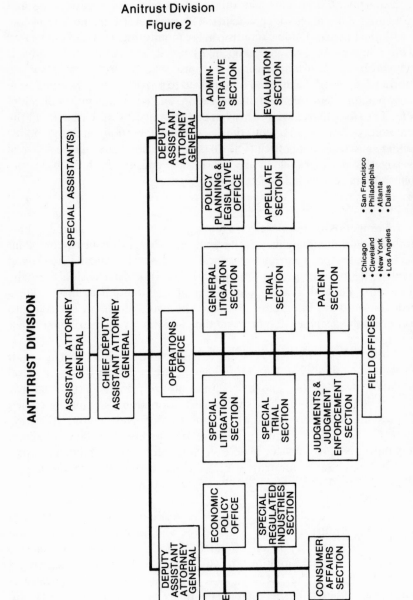

Source: 1976 Annual Report of the Attorney General of the United States.

the past wrongdoing but can do nothing to change future behavior or change the nature of the business or industry. Civil action, on the other hand, is taken when the division needs to stop an activity or change the nature of an industry or industry procedure (i.e., splitting a company that has a monopolistic position).

Civil and criminal cases can sometimes be expedited by accepting a plea of *nolo contendere*. Since the company does not contest the division's charges, the time and expense associated with lengthy litigation are avoided. Although a plea of *nolo contendere* is similar to a plea of guilty for sentencing purposes, it cannot be utilized as *prima facie* evidence of guilt in private treble damage suits. In other words, if companies that were damaged by the offender's action decide to sue for treble damages, they must collect evidence and prove in court the offender's guilt. If, on the other hand, the offender or court decides not to accept a consent order or *nolo contendere* plea and the government proves guilt in litigation, the outcome can subsequently be used by private businesses to sue the offender for treble damages. In addition, a plea of *nolo contendere* is sometimes advisable because the company may avoid extensive negative publicity during the trial period.

Advisory Opinion

Although the Antitrust Division has no formal procedure for developing and disseminating information concerning the division's attitude toward various activities, it periodically issues letters to requesting firms indicating current policy regarding a particular business activity. Many antitrust cases involving the Justice Department, however, involve complex and significant economic issues; in these cases, it is usually difficult to determine the legality of a situation with only cursory examination.

If the division does agree to cooperate by analyzing an activity, the business must provide them with all information relevant to the case. If, after reviewing the situation, the division feels that the activity is legal, it may waive its right to criminal prosecution. However, the division may still take civil action against the company. Also, if all facts are not presented to the government, it may proceed with either civil or criminal action.

Penalties

The Antitrust Division of the Department of Justice can seek the following penalties against firms for violating the law:
1. Structural remedies
2. Fines
3. Incarceration.

Structural remedies include dissolution, divorcement, and divestiture. Although there are technical differences between the three terms, in practice they mean essentially the same thing: to change the structure of a firm. Technically, dissolution means to dissolve an unlawful association between companies or groups. For example, in the Standard Oil case the court dissolved the association between Standard Oil Company of New Jersey (the holding company of an oil trust) and its subsidiaries. Divorcement represents "the result or upshot of a divestiture order."[11] Finally, divestiture means "undoing an anticompetitive situation by requiring the sale of some of the defendant firm's assets."[12]

Fines and incarceration are the two primary weapons the government has against criminal behavior. Violators of the Sherman Act may be subject to (1) a maximum jail term of three years, (2) a maximum corporate fine of $1 million, and (3) a maximum fine for the individuals involved of $100,000. Although courts have previously been reluctant to impose severe fines or prison sentences on violators of the Sherman Act, there is some indication that the trend will continue to change in the future. For example, during the mid-1970's approximately 36 paper product manufacturers were convicted of price fixing. Not only were they required to pay fines in excess of $1 million, but 14 of 59 convicted executives were sentenced to jail terms and the rest were fined or required to work on special service projects.[13]

Other Agencies and Statutes

Although the Federal Trade Commission and the Antitrust Division of the Department of Justice are primarily responsible for enforcing marketing law, there are dozens of other federal agencies that were established to protect consumers specifically from unsafe and unfair business activity.

Food and Drug Administration

The Food and Drug Administration was granted authority to enforce provisions of the Federal Food, Drug, and Cosmetics Act. It was also given authority to enforce the Caustic Poisons Act, which prohibits interstate shipment of caustic or dangerous substances, and it was given joint authority to regulate the Fair Packaging and Labeling Act. The FDA's primary

---

[10]Kenneth G. Elzinga and William Breit, *The Antitrust Penalties: A Study in Law and Economics,* Yale University Press (New Haven, 1976), p. 45.

[11]Elzinga and Breit.

[12]See: Timothy D. Schellhardt, "Pricing Fixing Charges Rise in Paper Industry Despite Convictions," *Wall Street Journal,* Vol. 61, No. 87 (May 4, 1978), p. 1.

activities include (1) controlling the misbranding of food, drugs, cosmetics, and therapeutic devices, (2) identifying and eliminating the adulteration of food, and (3) establishing standards of quality and identity. Some of the FDA's more significant activities are discussed in Chapter 6.

Consumer Product Safety Commission

The Consumer Product Safety Commission (CPSC) was established in 1972 to enforce the Consumer Product Safety Commission Act, Federal Hazardous Substances Act, Poison Packaging Prevention Act, Flammable Fabrics Act, and Refrigerator Safety Act. The CPSC's activities include (1) the identification of products which may be unsafe, (2) the development of labeling requirements and product safety standards, (3) the recall of products that are defective, (4) the banning of products that present an unreasonable risk of injury, and (5) the analysis of information on new products prior to their introduction into distribution channels. Extensive examination of the CPSC's authority, organizational structure, and remedies is presented in Chapter 6.

Department of Agriculture

The Department of Agriculture administers the Wholesome Meat Act, Poultry Products Inspection Act, Agricultural Marketing Act, Packers and Stockyards Act, Perishable Agricultural Commodities Act, and the Egg Products Inspection Act. Also to be discussed in Chapter 6, the Agriculture Department regulates the labeling of food, inspects meat processors, and develops quality and identity standards for meat and poultry.

Others

There are also numerous agencies that have significant power to regulate activities within a specified industry but generally have limited responsibility to control marketing practice. For example, deceptive practices by investment companies, air carriers, motor and rail carriers, alcoholic beverage manufacturers, and public utilities are regulated by the Securities and Exchange Commission, Civil Aeronautics Board, Interstate Commerce Commission, Treasury Department, and the Federal Power Commission, respectively.

In addition, the Federal Communications Commission is given authority to grant licenses to broadcast media and users of radio equipment and to develop standards of practice. The National Highway Traffic Safety Administration, a division of the Department of Transportation, is responsible for developing motor vehicle safety standards and monitoring the manufacture of motor vehicles in order to identify defects. Another agency, the Department of Commerce, helps companies develop voluntary product standards and works with business to develop consumer-oriented programs. The United States Postal Service is empowered to forbid fraudulent use of the mail and, therefore, regulate unfair direct sales practices. The Department of Housing and Urban Development was given authority by the Interstate Land Sales Full Disclosure Act—a law alleviating the sale of uninhabitable land to unwary consumers and requiring that developers register new subdivisions prior to making any interstate sale. Finally, the Office of Consumer Affairs, an agency of the Department of Health, Education, and Welfare, was established to inform consumers of the consumer-related activities of federal agencies and to interface between the Federal Government and consumers by distributing consumer complaints to ap-propriate agencies and advising federal agencies on consumer-related legislation and issues.

International Marketing Law

Cultivation and penetration of international markets has become an attractive growth strategy for American as well as foreign firms. As companies began to saturate domestic markets, ventures into other geographical areas expanded the marketer's potential and relieved pressures to stimulate heavier usage of existing market segments. For many firms, expansion into international markets proved to be very rewarding, and they have begun to envision penetration of these markets as a primary rather than secondary objective. In other words, rather than simply use foreign markets to extend the life cycle of products that reached the decline stage, firms aggressively cultivated these markets during introductory periods.

The political response of the U.S. Government suggests that they correctly envision the trend toward international business to continue. Not only has the Government expanded the scope of international regulations, but they have changed the Tariff Commission (now known as the International Trade Commission) to enable it to monitor and regulate international business practice effectively.

This section will briefly introduce the laws that influence international marketing activity. Although all significant aspects of international marketing law will be discussed, extensive examination of the numerous sections of the laws is beyond the scope of this text.

International Trade Commission

With its name change from the U.S. Tariff Commission, the International Trade Commission (ITC) assumed a new role. As the Tariff Commission, its primary function was to handle tariffs, the primary regulatory tool of international trade. As the tariff's role as an instrument of international trade began to change, however, the Commission's authority and responsibility had to experience corresponding change. The new International Trade Commission assumed a regulatory position similar to that enjoyed by the FTC. Specifically, the ITC can evaluate and determine the legality of activities, identify the impact of trade practices on business and consumers, issue cease and desist orders, and ban products from domestic distribution.

Antidumping

Product dumping involves selling a product in a foreign country for a lower price than the price charged in the seller's own country. Considered to be the equivalent of price discrimination, the impact of dumping on the importing country is as follows:

(1) In the short run, dumping reduces prices to consumers of the importing country.

(2) The lower prices exert pressure on competitors in the importing country to meet the lower prices.

(3) Competition is reduced because of the competitors' inability to meet low prices initiated by the foreign exporter.

(4) In the long run, the reduction in competition will be accompanied by higher prices.

To restrict foreign firms from dumping products on U.S. markets at lower than competitive prices, Congress enacted the Revenue Act of 1916. The law basically made it unlawful for an exporter to intentionally attempt to destroy competition by selling a product in the U.S. for a price which is lower than the product's market value in the exporting country plus duties, freight, and other expenses. Since "intent to injure" U.S. companies is extremely difficult to prove, the Act of 1916 has never successfully been applied.

To alleviate problems of proving "intent," Congress enacted the Antidumping Act of 1921 which did not require that "intent to injure" be proven. The Treasury Department was given authority to charge a duty for products that were sold for a lower price in the U.S. than in their own country.

As other countries began to understand the negative long-run implications of dumping, they took steps similar to the U.S. to restrict its development. In addition to enacting their own statutes, other countries have joined the U.S. in developing an International Antidumping Code. In essence, the code delineates activities that may result in dumping provisions being applied.

Trade Act of 1974

A significant change in attitudes toward international trade was indicated by passage of the 1974 Trade Act. In essence, the act expanded the scope of international marketing legislation and gave the government more authority to encourage trade between countries. In expanding the scope of legislation, the law made it unlawful for a company which is importing goods into the U.S. to engage in unfair methods of competition which tend to destroy or injure U.S. industry or prevent the establishment of such an industry. If the International Trade Commission finds that an activity is, in fact, injurious to American industry, it may ban the firm's products from domestic distribution. The predominant unfair practice successfully challenged by the government has been patent infringement.

Another primary objective of the Trade Act is facilitating international trade activity by reducing legislative barriers imposed by antidumping legislation. This was partially accomplished by authorizing the President to enter into agreements with foreign nations to reduce import duties. In addition to requiring that the President discuss trade plans with the International Trade Commission, representatives from all sectors of society can participate in the development of agreements by giving advice at various levels of negotiation.

Webb-Pomerene Export Trade Act

Passed in 1918 to enable U.S. manufacturers to compete in international markets, the Webb-Pomerene Act allows firms to unite for the purpose of engaging in export trade. Although the resultant voluntary association can assist its members in exporting activities, it cannot use its power to affect prices within the U.S., restrain trade by fixing prices with foreign competitors, or divide territories collusively. Also, a new association of exporters must file with the FTC within 30 days of formation.

Sherman, Clayton, and FTC Acts

The Sherman Act declares that "every contract, combination, . . . or conspiracy, in restraint of trade or commerce among the several states, or with foreign nations, is hereby declared illegal." The law applies to all restraints that have a significant effect on commerce within the U.S. The contract can take place between U.S. firms, between U.S. and foreign firms, in U.S. territory, or in foreign territory. For example, if exporting firms join together to decide on prices to be charged in a foreign country, the activity is illegal. If, on the other hand, the activity does not have an impact on U.S. commerce, it is legal. For example, restricting an agent or distributor to one country or territory would probably have inconsequential impact on U.S. commerce and, therefore, would not be considered illegal.

The FTC and Clayton Acts also have jurisdiction in international trade activity. Although unfair practices in both export and import trade are regulated by the FTC Act, only import trade is regulated by the Clayton Act. For example, a merger between a foreign and domestic firm may be evaluated under Section 7 of the Clayton Act, utilizing the same criteria as if the firms were both domestic. If the foreign firm does not engage in commerce within the U.S., however, Clayton Act provisions would not apply.[14] It could possibly be attached under the Sherman Act if the intent of the merger were to restrain competition.

Antibribery

One aspect of international trade which has recently received significant attention from both domestic and foreign governments is bribery of foreign officials by U.S. corporations. Not only did the bribery activity receive considerable attention because of the ethical and moral issues surrounding such business practice, but it was a widespread activity that permeated all sectors of the business community. In fact, 117 of the Fortune 500 firms combined with over 300 other firms to make over $300 million in questionable or illegal payments to foreign officials.[15]

Since federal and state bribery laws only apply to payments of U.S. officials, Congress enacted another statute, the Foreign Corrupt Practices Act of 1977, to restrain such activity. In essence, the Foreign Corrupt Practices Act makes it a criminal offense to offer or pay a foreign official to help a company obtain or maintain business with a foreign government. Violators of the law are subject to a corporate fine of up to $1 million, an individual fine of up to $10,000, and a prison sentence of 5 years.

One of the primary problems with the law is its impact on U.S. corporations' ability to compete effectively in foreign markets. Since bribery of officials is legal and customary in some foreign markets, prohibition of this tool places U.S. corporations at a significant competitive disadvantage. It also restricts a company's ability to protect its overseas investments from arbitrary government restrictions, takeover, or expulsion.

State Law

There are also state laws that protect business and consumers from unscrupulous practices of business. Because of the limited resources and, in

[13]Unless the foreign firm was a "toehold" firm: See Chapter 3 for "toehold" mergers.

[14]Gerald T. McLaughlin, "The Criminalization Foreign Payments by Corporations: A Comparative Legal Systems Analysis," *Fordham Law Review,* Vol. 46, (May, 1978), p. 1072.

some cases, limited jurisdiction of the FTC and Department of Justice, the state regulators serve an important supplementary function.[16] Although many of the state statutes, such as Unfair Trade Practice Act, Consumer Protection Act, and Printers' Ink Statute, are model laws to be adopted in similar form by most states, there are also many laws dealing with pricing, distribution, and other practices. Because of the diversity of law in various states, an extensive examination of each state's law is beyond the scope of the text. There will be an extensive examination of state law, however, in cases where the state is the primary regulatory agent (i.e., in cases of strict liability).

Exemptions From the Antitrust Statutes

Although most industries must operate within the constraints of the antitrust laws, several industries and groups have sought and received immunity from the various marketing laws. In addition to the groups that have been exempted from antitrust coverage, several other industries are at least partially exempt from FTC or Department of Justice regulation but are regulated by another designated government agency. As was indicated in the previous section, the Federal Communications Commission regulates activities of the communication industry, the Securities and Exchange Commission regulates the securities industry, the Federal Power Commission regulates the electric and gas companies, the Civil Aeronautics Board regulates air carriers, and the Interstate Commerce Commission controls the transportation industry.

Agricultural cooperatives and associations received specific immunity from antitrust statutes in Section 6 of the Clayton Act, which states that "nothing contained in the antitrust laws shall be construed to forbid the existence and operation of labor, agricultural, or horticultural organizations, instituted for the purposes of mutual help . . . nor shall such organizations or members thereof be held or construed to be illegal combinations or conspiracies in restraint of trade . . . ." In 1922, the Capper-Volstead Act specifically approved all agricultural associations except those that monopolized or restrained trade "to such an extent that the price . . . is unduly enhanced." Also, the Cooperative Marketing Act of 1926 authorized the exchange of pricing and market data among the various associations. Finally, the practice of returning savings to cooperative members was exempted from regulation by Section 4 of the Robinson-Patman Act.

---

[15]See Chapter 3 for a discussion of the commerce requirement.

Other exemptions from the Federal Antitrust Laws include the following:

• *Organized Labor* (i.e., Section 20 of the Clayton Act and the Norris-LaGuardia Act)—Organized labor is exempt from laws regulating boycotting and strikes but is prevented from conspiring to fix prices, divide markets, or boycott other employers.

• *International Trade*—The Webb-Pomerene Act of 1918 exempts from antitrust regulation some cooperative activities between exporters as long as the association is designed to promote foreign trade and not to lessen competition within the United States.

• *Small Business*—The Small Business Act authorized the Small Business Administration to encourage small businesses to cooperate among themselves in various research and business activities.

• *Insurance Companies*—Enacted in 1945, the McCarran-Ferguson Act exempted companies that are engaged in insurance activities from Federal jurisdiction in favor of state regulation.

Summary

Marketing is a complex system of business activities designed to plan, promote, and distribute goods and services to ultimate consumers and industrial users. Although most marketers ethically engage in product planning, pricing, promotion, and distribution activities according to the rules of free enterprise, some marketers find it profitable to deviate from the rules to satisfy their own selfish interests. Widespread practice of such deviate behavior as price fixing, predatory pricing, division of markets, and rebating eventually placed free enterprise in a vulnerable position. Small business and the competitive environment were slowly being replaced by the monopolization of entire industries.

To reverse the trend toward monopolization, Congress enacted the Sherman Antitrust Act of 1890, which declared illegal every contract, combination, and conspiracy in restraint of trade as well as monopolies and attempts to monopolize. In addition to regulating monopolies directly, the Government also decided that it was necessary to control activities which, if practiced, could give impetus to reduction in competition and the development of monopolies. Therefore, in 1914 Congress enacted the Clayton Act which was designed to control price discrimination, tying contracts, exclusive deals, and mergers. Also in 1914 it passed the FTC Act in order to establish a commission (the Federal Trade Commission) for regulating unfair competitive behavior and unfair methods of competition.

During the 1920's and 1930's the business environment underwent some significant changes. Retail chains evolved into large-scale buying powers capable of demanding discriminatory price reductions and advertising support from manufacturers. Communication systems improved, encouraging mass advertising and its accompanying deceptive techniques. In addition, improvements in man-made fibers made deceptive labeling of furs and wool products a reality. Congress, therefore, passed (1) the Robinson-Patman Act (1936) to amend the Clayton Act and partially neutralize buying advantages of retail chains, (2) the Wheeler-Lea Act (1938) to amend the FTC Act and give the FTC power to control business practice and protect rights of consumers, and (3) a series of labeling laws to alleviate misbranding.

During the 1950's and 1960's as consumer affluence became a reality and consumer behavior reflected a "live-for-today" attitude, indiscriminate purchasing and extensive use of credit became the norm. To prevent business from unethically exploiting these indiscriminate and, in many cases, ignorant shoppers, Congress enacted numerous "consumer right to know/consumer protection" laws. Some of these were Fair Packaging and Labeling, Truth in Lending, Fair Credit Reporting, Consumer Product Safety, Fair Credit Billing, FTC Improvement—Magnuson-Moss Warranty, Equal Credit Opportunity, Consumer Product Safety Commission Improvement, and Fair Debt Collection Practice Acts.

In addition to these Federal domestic laws, which are designed to regulate interstate commerce, there are also laws designed to regulate intrastate commerce and international trade. Intrastate commerce is regulated by individual state laws such as the various unfair trade practice acts and consumer protection acts. International trade is regulated by the International Trade Commission and the various laws designed to (1) protect American business from unfair practices of foreign firms and (2) give American exporters certain exemptions from domestic law so they can effectively compete in foreign markets.

Discussion Questions

1. From an economic perspective, should monopolies be regulated by antitrust laws? Why? Specifically identify economic theories to support your argument.

2. The goal of antitrust law is to help maintain a strong competitive environment. Does this "preservation of competition" objective suggest that the government also help preserve individual competitors?

3. Should labor unions be exempt from antitrust legislation?

4. Would elimination of antitrust laws have a positive or negative effect on competition?

5. Has U.S. public policy relative to product dumping been effective in protecting American business from illegal practices of foreign business? Cite example.

6. What changes would you make to strengthen present marketing law?

2 DISTRIBUTION CHANNEL RELATIONSHIPS

In order to facilitate the exchange of goods and services effectively and efficiently, it is mandatory that the marketer develop, coordinate, and maintain an efficient distribution channel framework. This channel framework consists of a series of channel members and facilitating agencies, and it is sensitive to social, economic, and political interrelationships which significantly influence channel performance. Before channel systems can be designed and techniques for managing and controlling the complex system of channel activities can be established, however, one must consider the various contingencies which constrain their full implementation.

Legally, although the Sherman Act has been utilized to monitor channel activity, it can only be applied when the activity involves monopolization, an attempt to monopolize, or conspiracies to restrain trade unreasonably. Because of this limitation it has been somewhat ineffective in checking most distribution channel activities. The Clayton Act, on the other hand, was designed specifically to regulate the numerous channel activities which were beyond the scope of the Sherman Act. Specifically, the Clayton Act prohibits exclusive dealing contracts, tying contracts, requirement contracts, reciprocal arrangements, mergers, and joint ventures where there is an incipient threat that the arrangement will lessen competition or tend to create a monopoly.

In light of these channel topics, this chapter focuses on and explores two specific areas:

(1) The various intrachannel and interchannel management practices and the profound impact that the legal contingency has on the nature and scope of these management practices.

(2) The court's thinking relative to these activities as well as several additional restraints which are regulated by the Sherman Act (i.e., horizontal and vertical market divisions).

28

Exclusive Dealing Contracts

Exclusive dealing contracts involve situations where the seller agrees to sell only through one agency and the agency reciprocates by agreeing to sell the product of only one manufacturer. Exclusive agreements have advantages for both the buyer and the seller. On the one hand, the contract gives the seller a readily-available market. Second, the seller's distribution, inventory, promotion, and production costs are reduced because of the certainty surrounding demand for the seller's product. Finally, by obtaining an agreement from the agency to refrain from selling competing products, all dealer efforts are directed toward marketing the seller's product.

The buyer also benefits from the exclusive agency arrangement. First, if the buyer must invest in salespeople, parts, service, and facilities, he does not want competing agencies benefiting from this investment. Second, the buyer is assured of receiving an adequate supply. Third, if the seller obtains agreement from all agencies to sell only in their assigned territories, the agencies do not have to worry about competition among themselves. Finally, by agreeing to sell only one product, inventories of other products are eliminated, thus reducing total inventory costs.

The legality of exclusive agreements and the advantages resulting from the arrangements are dealt with in Section 3 of the Clayton Act, Section 5 of the Federal Trade Commission Act, and Section 1 of the Sherman Act. The relevant part of Section 3 of the Clayton Act says that:

It shall be unlawful for any person engaged in commerce to lease or make a sale or contract for sale of goods on the condition that the lessee or purchaser shall not deal in the goods of a competitor of the lessor or seller where the effect may be to substantially lessen competition or tend to create a monopoly.

Section 5 of the Federal Trade Commission Act attacks exclusive arrangements which are "unfair methods of competition." Finally, Section 1 declares that "every contract, combination or conspiracy in restraint of trade is illegal."

Although exclusive dealing contracts are not illegal *per se*, they are normally considered illegal if (1) the manufacturer's sales volume represents a substantial percent of the total sales volume for a particular product class in the affected market or (2) competition is substantially lessened because the dealer who is involved in the exclusive deal has a dominant position in the market. In other words, if a dealer has a significant share of market and only one manufacturer can sell to that dealer, then penetration of that market is virtually closed to competing manufacturers.

The illegality of a dominant manufacturer coercing an independent dealer to handle only the dominant manufacturer's inventory (condition 1 above) was established early in the development of antitrust law. Standard Fashion Company, a manufacturer of paper clothing patterns, required that its dealers maintain a sufficient inventory of the patterns and not handle the patterns of competing manufacturers. Since Standard Fashion maintained exclusive distribution in 40 percent of U.S. pattern dealers, there was a significant lessening of competition.[1]

Similarly, the legality of exclusive dealings contracts was delineated in the Standard Oil of California Case.[2] Standard Oil required that its dealers carry only Standard's tires, oil, gasoline, and accessories. The court found that the agreement which confined the dealers to only Standard's products was an unreasonable restraint of trade in violation of the Sherman Act. Also, the exclusive agreement resulted in a substantial lessening of competition, in violation of Section 3 of the Clayton Act, even though the amount of foreclosed competition only equaled 7 percent of the area's retail sales.

The primary test applied by the courts in the Standard Oil Case and other subsequent cases was the "quantitative substantiality" test. In other words, if an exclusive contract forecloses a substantial share of the market to competition, the contract is an unreasonable restraint of trade and, therefore, is illegal. Since Standard sold 23 percent of the gasoline marketed in the Western states and had exclusive contracts with 16 percent of the retail outlets accounting for approximately 7 percent of the area's gasoline sales, the amount of commerce affected was substantial. "Quantitative substantiality" can, therefore, relate to situations where (1) the manufacturer controls a substantial share of the market (i.e., 23 percent of gasoline sales) or (2) the buyer has a dominant position (i.e., 16 percent of the area's retail outlets). Also, if the substantiality test is confirmed, "rule of reason considerations are not applicable,"[3] and it is unnecessary to prove the effects of the contract on competition.

Tying Contracts

A tying contract is a situation in which the seller agrees to sell one product, the tying product, only if the buyer agrees to buy the seller's other product(s), the tied product(s).

There are several conditions which often make tying arrangements an attractive marketing strategy for sellers.

[1]*Standard Fashion Company v. Magrane Housfon Company* 258 U.S. 346, (1922).
[2]*Standard Oil Company of California v. United States,* 337 U.S. 293 (1949).
[3]Samuel Weisbard, "Resale Price Maintenance, Exclusive Dealing, and Tying Arrangements," *The Antitrust Bulletin,* Vol. 10, No. 3 (May-June 1965), pp. 367-368.

(1) The seller has an attractive (i.e., high quality, low price) product that the buyer must have to compete with other dealers. Purchase of the attractive product, however, is contingent upon the dealer's agreement to purchase the weaker product also (i.e., low quality, high price). If the buyer must purchase the seller's entire line to obtain the tying product, the practice is called "full-line forcing."

(2) The seller has patented equipment or a copyrighted product necessary to the buyer. The seller, therefore, ties the patented item to other unpatented products offered by the seller (tie-in arrangements).

(3) The seller is also a franchisor and ties the purchase of products needed in the operation of the franchise to the purchase of the franchise.

All tying arrangements can be subject to prosecution under Section 3 of the Clayton Act if competition relative to the tied product is substantially lessened. The practice can also violate Section 1 of the Sherman Act and Section 5 of the Federal Trade Commission Act. Although tying arrangements are not *per se* violations of these laws, the courts have expressed their concern that tying contracts serve no purpose other than the suppression of competition.[4]

Full-line forcing and tying agreements which do not involve patents, copyrights, or franchises (condition 1 above) are normally illegal unless the tying product is neither unique nor attractive enough to restrain competition in the tied market.[5] These types of tying contracts are always illegal if the buyer is precluded from purchasing the tying product from other buyers or "the seller has sufficient economic power with respect to the tying product to restrain free competition appreciably in the market for the tied product."[6] It is also important to know that "economic power with respect to the tying product" can result from simply owning an attractive brand (i.e., tying product) that dealers must have because of consumer demand. For example, in one case a cemetery tied the purchase of lots (tying product) to the purchase of markers and lot care service (tied product). The Court of Appeals indicated that the practice violated the law because the tying product had "uniqueness and desirability" and competition was significantly restrained in the tied market.[7] The result of this case, as well as numerous other cases dealing with tying contracts, is to warn companies against

[4]*Standard Oil Company of California v. U.S.,* 337 U.S. 293 (1949).

[5]See: *Arlie Mack Moore et. al. v. Jas. H. Matthews & Co., Rest Haven Memorial Association et. al.,* "Legal Developments in Marketing," *Journal of Marketing,* Vol. 41, No. 4 (October 1977), p. 108.

[6]Lee N. Abrams, "Tying Arrangements and Exclusive Dealing Contracts," *Chicago Bar Record,* Vol. 53, No. 2 (November 1971) p. 76; also, *Northern Pacific Railway Co. v. United States,* 356 U.S. 1 (1958).

[7]*Arlie Mack Moore, et. al.*

developing such agreements under almost any circumstance.[8] Although they are not illegal *per se,* judicial precedent would suggest that the only acceptable tying arrangements are those surrounded by extremely unusual circumstances.

Condition 2 (using a patented product as the tying product) has been declared illegal in almost all cases. For example, International Salt Company was found guilty of violating Section 3 of the Clayton Act and the Sherman Act by leasing patented salt machines (lixator and saltomats) on the condition that the lessee would purchase all salt from International Salt.[9] The contract prevented the lessee from purchasing salt in the open market at a lower price. If a significant amount of competition is foreclosed by this type of tie-in arrangement, then the contract is illegal *per se.*

A similar case was brought against the American Can Company in the early 1950's.[10] American Can Company leased its patented can closing equipment to canners only if they were willing to buy their cans from American Can. This type of arrangement restricts competition between American Can and any other canner for the business of the lessee of the equipment. Therefore, it was in violation of the Sherman and Clayton Acts.[11]

As suggested in Condition 3, franchising provides the franchisor (seller of the franchise) with an opportunity to tie certain items which are used by the franchisee (independent businessman) for operating the business to the purchase of the franchise. This practice is illegal unless such contracts are necessary in order to control quality standards or protect trade secrets. Consistency of quality among all franchisers is, of course, one of the primary advantages of franchising. A person can purchase Kentucky Fried Chicken at a Dallas franchise, and it will taste exactly like chicken purchased at a Kentucky Fried Chicken franchise in Miami. Without this quality control the franchise system would lose one of its primary benefits for the consumer.

On the other hand, the franchisee is an independent business person and, therefore, should have the opportunity to operate the business at optimum efficiency. Having the flexibility to purchase standard quality supplies at the lowest price is necessary in order to maximize profits and

---

[8]*U.S. v. Paramount Pictures, Inc.,* 334 U.S. 131 (1948); *U.S. v. Loew's, Inc.,* 371 U.S. 38 (1962). The companies offered desirable films only if the theater accepted an agreement to lease other, less desirable films (i.e., block booking). They were also illegal because the less desirable films drew on the quality and individuality of the desirable films.

[9]*International Salt Company, Inc. v. U.S.,* 332 U.S. 392, (1947).

[10]*U.S. v. American Can Company et. al.,* 87 F. Supp. 18 (1949).

[11]For additional discussion of tying arrangements and patented products, see Donald Turner, "The Validity of Tying Arrangements Under the Antitrust Laws," *Harvard Law Review,* Vol. 72, No. 1 (November 1958), pp. 50-75.

return. Therefore, a Chicken Delight franchisee should be allowed to purchase chicken from any independent chicken producer if chicken quality is consistent with the franchisor's quality specifications. Otherwise, competition is restricted between the franchisor and other chicken producers for the franchisee's business.[12]

In summary, tying arrangements are illegal in all but the unusual circumstances. Since they are not illegal *per se,* the court must consider the following questions in each case to ascertain legal status:

(1) Can the seller significantly restrain competition in the tied market with economic power realized from sale of the tying product?

(2) Do two distinct, separate products types exist (a tying and tied product)?

(3) Is a significant amount of commerce affected by the tying contract?[13]

There are also several situations which, if present, may serve as justification for the tying contract:

(1) No economic power exists because the tying product is not sufficiently unique.

(2) The tying contract is necessary to control the quality image of the tying product (i.e., in some franchising operations).

(3) Two distinct products do not exist; for example, the Times-Picayune Publishing Company published both a morning and evening newspaper. In order to purchase advertising space in one of the editions, one had to buy space in the other edition. The court ruled that the products (morning and evening editions) and markets were the same and, therefore, there was no dominant tying product which gave the publisher economic leverage in the tied market.[14]

(4) The "use of the tying product is essential to the efficient operation of the tied product."[15]

Requirements Contracts

Another arrangement directly related to exclusive dealing is the requirements contract. The agreement maintains that the buyer must buy or

[12]*H. Siegal et. al. v. Chicken Delight et. al.,* 448 F 2d 43 (1971).

[13]See: Stephen J. Smirti, Jr., "Trademarks as Tying Products: The Presumption of Economic Power," *St. Johns Law Review,* Vol. 50, No. 4 (Summer 1976), pp. 689-723.

[14]*Times-Picayune Publishing Co. v. United States,* 345 U.S. 594 (1953); also see Malcolm E. Wheeler, "Some Observations on Tie-ins, the Single-Product Defense, Exclusive Dealing and Regulated Industries," *California Law Review,* Vol. 60, No. 6 (November 1972), pp. 1558-1562.

[15]Abrams, p. 78.

lease all or part of its requirements from one seller for a specified time period. Oftentimes, it is difficult to differentiate a tying contract and a requirements contract. In fact, the American Can case is often referred to as an example of a requirements agreement because the buyers were required to buy all of their cans from American on a long-term contract. However, since the purchase of the cans was tied to the purchase of canning equipment, it is generally considered a tying agreement.

The primary advantage of the requirements contract is that the buyer is assured of a continuous source of supply. For the seller, it alleviates competition for the contracted buyer's business. Also, the seller can plan future sales more effectively which, of course, facilitates production planning.

Any requirements contract may violate the Sherman Act, Section 3 of the Clayton Act, or Section 5 of the Federal Trade Commission Act. They are not illegal *per se*, but may be considered illegal if they restrain trade or substantially lessen competition. Therefore, it is necessary to apply the "rule of reason" to each case.[16] In other words, whether or not a contract is an unreasonable restraint of trade depends upon economic implications of the activity.

Two cases illustrate the thinking of the courts concerning requirements contracts. In the first case, Linde Air Products Company was found guilty of violating Section 3 of the Clayton Act.[17] For approximately eleven years, Linde Air Products held and licensed a patent for the Unionmelt Welding Process. In addition, Linde sold the rods used in the process to the licensees. If the licensees agreed to purchase their entire requirements from Linde, they received a half-cent per pound discount. The court found that the discount, coupled with the requirements contract, lessened competition substantially between Linde and other "rod" manufacturers.

A case which illustrates a situation where requirements contracts are legal involves an electric utility company and a supplier of bituminous coal.[18] The mining company entered into a twenty-year contract to supply the electric company with approximately one million tons of coal annually. Shortly after Tampa Electric developed the burners to utilize the coal as fuel, the mining company advised them that the contract violated the antitrust laws and would not be performed. Subsequently, Tampa Electric sued the mining company, contending that the contract was valid. The Supreme Court found that the lessening of competition in the relevant market was insubstantial since the maximum volume of coal product in-

---

[16]*Standard Oil of New Jersey et al. v. U.S.*, 221 U.S. 1 (1911).
[17]*U.S. v. Linde Air Products Company*, 83 F. Supp. 978 (1949).
[18]*Tampa Electric Company v. Nashville Coal Company*, 365 U.S. 320 (1961).

volved was only .77 percent of the total amount of coal produced and marketed in the relevant market.

The result of the Tampa Electric case was twofold. First, it reemphasized that an exclusive dealing contract (including requirements contract) is illegal only "if it forecloses competition in a substantial share of the market."[19] Second, the Tampa Electric decision modified the "Quantitative Substantiality" test applied in the Standard Oil Case. Instead of simply relying on quantitative market share or sales information to establish unreasonableness, the courts must also consider the probable effect of the contract on competition. Whether or not competition is reduced depends upon (1) the relative strength of the parties, (2) the ratio of commerce covered by the contract to the total volume in the relevant market, and (3) the effect of the contract on competition.[20]

Reciprocity

Reciprocity involves a situation where Buyer A agrees to buy from Buyer B only if Buyer B agrees to reciprocate by purchasing from Buyer A. In other words, "if you will buy from me, I will buy from you." According to Moyer, there are several advantages of using reciprocity.[21] First, it reduces selling costs because of the minimum of selling effort required. Second, costs of searching for sources of supply and outlets for merchandise disposal are reduced.

Although reciprocity is a widely-accepted method of conducting business, it is not immune from examination by the courts. As with other forms of exclusive agreements, reciprocity can be attacked under the Sherman Act, Section 3 of the Clayton Act, or Section 5 of the Federal Trade Commission Act.

In the early 1960's, General Motors was accused in both criminal and civil court of utilizing its size and related bargaining power to exert pressure on railroads to engage in a reciprocal agreement.[22] General Motors formed a subsidiary company which manufactured locomotives. Because of the volume of business General Motors transacted with the railroads, it could force the railroads to purchase its locomotives by threatening to ship

---

[19]Abrams, pp. 80-81.

[20]365 U.S. 320 (1961).

[21]Reed Moyer, "Reciprocity: Retrospect and Prospect," *Journal of Marketing,* Vol. 34, No. 4 (October 1970), p. 52.

[22]*U.S. v. General Motors Corporation,* Criminal Action 61-CR-365 (April 12, 1961); *U.S. v. General Motors Corporation,* Civil Action 63C80 (January 14, 1963).

through other railroads if competing locomotives were purchased. As a result of the conspiracy, General Motors captured 84 percent of the locomotive business. The courts found the activity in violation of the Clayton and Sherman Acts and sought divestiture of the locomotive division by General Motors. Anticompetitive reciprocity, therefore, involves a situation where one firm can use its market strength to coerce companies into compliance with the reciprocal agreement.

The courts have also taken a position against organized reciprocity. Organized reciprocity utilizes a trade relations department which gathers information on suppliers from the purchasing department, then provides the marketing department with the information. The marketing department subsequently uses this information as a selling tool to encourage the supplier to engage in a reciprocal purchasing agreement. Since the courts began questioning the utilization of trade relations departments to collect and disseminate purchasing and marketing information, the departments have all but disappeared.[23]

Finally, conglomerate mergers may, in some cases, facilitate reciprocity. For example, in 1951 Consolidated Foods—a large producer, distributor, and retailer of foods—acquired Gentry, Inc., a producer of dehydrated onion and garlic.[24] Immediately prior to the acquisition, Gentry controlled approximately a 28 percent share of the market for dehydrated onions and 51 percent for garlic; their primary competitor, Basic Vegetables Products, Inc., had 60 percent of the onion market and 39 percent of the garlic market. By 1958, Gentry had 35 percent of the onion market and only 39 percent of the garlic market. The FTC challenged the merger because it gave Gentry an avenue for coercing food processors into buying the Gentry product while competitors had no similar bargaining position. Since Consolidated Foods purchased large quantities of food from processors that used dehydrated onions and garlic in food preparation, they could suggest that the processor purchase their onion and garlic needs from Gentry or cease to be a supplier for Consolidated. Consolidated eventually did put such pressure on suppliers and was successful in drawing business from Basic to Gentry, despite the fact that Basic had a superior product. Also, the FTC indicated that Gentry's share of garlic sales would have probably fallen more than 12 percent without the merger.

Consequently, the FTC considered the merger to be in violation of the

[23]F. Robert Finney, "Reciprocity: Gone But Not Forgotten," *Journal of Marketing,* Vol. 42, No. 1 (January 1978), pp. 55-56; also, K. A. Hinnegan, "Potential Reciprocity and the Conglomerate Merger: Consolidated Foods Revisited," *Buffalo Law Review,* Vol. 17, No. 2 (Winter 1968), pp. 633-637.

[24]*FTC v. Consolidated Foods Corp.,* 380 U.S. 592 (1965).

Clayton Act by substantially lessening competition between Gentry and other producers of dehydrated onions and garlic. Specifically, Commissioner Elman indicated that reciprocal arrangements are anticompetitive and should be treated as *per se* violations when he said that "it distorts the focus of the trader by interposing between him and the traditional competitive factors of price, quality, and service an irrelevant and alien factor which is destructive of fair and free competition on the basis of merit."[25] Although the Supreme Court did not rule that reciprocity is illegal *per se*, the court upheld the FTC's decision and indicated that reciprocity which results from a merger is illegal if there is the probability that competition is lessened.

Vertical Merger

The vertical merger involves the purchase of assets or stock of a channel member. For instance, a manufacturer may find it advisable to buy a retailer or wholesaler in order to gain access to the market (forward vertical integration). Also, a manufacturer may integrate with a producer to insure uninterrupted supply of some resource which is vital to manufacturing operations (backward vertical integration). Backward vertical integration can also be accomplished by a retailer or wholesaler who purchases the assets or stock of a higher channel member.

Vertical mergers can be condemned as an attempt to monopolize under Section 2 of the Sherman Act or as an attempt to restrain trade substantially under Section 7 of the Clayton Act as amended by the Celler-Kefauver Amendment (1950). Since a company must approach monopolistic power to be condemned under the Sherman Act, it has been ineffective in controlling mergers. This is evidenced by the fact that more corporate mergers took place during the 2 decades immediately following passage of the Sherman Act than in any period in American history.[26]

The Sherman Act's weakness in attacking mergers was further suggested by the Supreme Court in *United States v. Columbia Steel Company.*[27] U.S. Steel produced semi-manufactured rolled-steel products which were subsequently used to produce structural steel and plate products. In an attempt to enter the Western market, they acquired Consolidated Steel Corporation—a fabricating company involved with processing semi-manufactured steel. Since the acquisition would cause Consolidated to purchase

---

[25]*FTC v. Consolidated Foods,* Docket #7000, 1961.

[26]David Dale Martin, *Mergers and the Clayton Act,* University of California Press (Berkeley, 1959), p. 14.

[27]*U.S. v. Columbia Steel Company,* 334 U.S. 495 (1948).

all semi-manufactured steel requirements from U. S. Steel, the arrangement eliminated competition between U. S. Steel and all other companies for Consolidated's business.[28] The courts ruled in favor of the steel companies because the merger was an efficient commercial activity designed to enter the Western market and not an attempt to foreclose competition and create a monopoly. Therefore, the result was "when the largest company . . . was allowed to purchase its largest 'steel fabrication' competitor, it became evident that the Sherman Act did not forbid a merger unless the merging firms were on the verge of obtaining substantial monopoly power."[29]

Section 7 of the Clayton Act has, therefore, been the most effective legal device for regulating anticompetitive mergers. The law, as amended by the Celler-Kefauver Act, condemns mergers which may substantially lessen competition or tend to create a monopoly. Since only a reasonable probability of injury to competition is required, it is necessary to show intent to monopolize or restrain trade.

In essence, the legality of a vertical merger depends upon the effect of the merger on competition in the relevant markets. The thinking of the courts with respect to vertical mergers is indicated in a case involving the merger between Brown Shoe Company, the fourth largest shoe manufacturer, and Kinney Shoes, the largest independent chain of family shoe stores.[30] The procedure of the courts is to (1) identify the relevant product market, (2) identify the relevant geographic market, and (3) examine the effect of the merger on this relevant market. The relevant product market is identified by examining the following factors: industry or public recognition of the submarket as a separate economic entity, the product's peculiar characteristics, unique production facilities, distinct customers, distinct prices, sensitivity to price changes, and specialized vendors. The Supreme Court identified the relevant product as men's, women's, and children's shoes. In addition, since the two companies were capable of penetrating any geographical market, the relevant geographical market was the nation.

After identifying the relevant product and geographic markets, the court evaluated the consequences of the vertical merger on competition. The important factors affecting the decision were as follows:

(1) The purpose of the merger from the manufacturer's perspective was to force its shoes into Kinney's stores.

(2) The merger could possibly lead to other mergers in the industry and therefore establish a trend toward vertical integration.

---

[28]See: A. D. Neal, *The Antitrust Laws of the United States,* Cambridge University Press (Cambridge, 1960), pp. 143-154.

[29]Ernest Gellhorn, *Antitrust Law and Economics in a Nutshell,* West Publishing Company (St. Paul, 1976), p. 302.

[30]*Brown Shoe Company v. United States,* 370 U.S. 294 (1962).

(3) Competition for Kinney's business was foreclosed because of Brown's policy of forcing shoes into Kinney's outlets.

(4) No countervailing competitive, economic, or social advantages were created by the merger.

Since the merger substantially lessened competition and established a trend toward vertical integration in the shoe industry, it was declared illegal.

Horizontal Merger

The horizontal merger involves the purchase of assets or stock of a company on the same level of distribution selling the same product line.

Instead of expanding internally by cultivating new markets, some companies find it expedient to acquire a competitor and realize both market penetration and the elimination of a competitor. Also, the merging organization can oftentimes achieve these marketing objectives much faster than would be possible through internal expansion. Timely expansion of markets can be vitally important in numerous industries, especially in high-technology industrial organizations where there is often a high correlation between market share dominance and profitability. Realization of market dominance early in the growth stage of the product life cycle may be the key to subsequent long-run growth and survival.

Although there are numerous reasons why companies desire market expansion through horizontal integration, the court is primarily concerned with the effect of the merger on competition, the market shares of the merging companies, and current as well as future trends toward concentration in the industry and not on the internal achievements of the firms. The court has taken a definite, strong position against mergers involving additional industry concentration. For example, the FTC issued a guideline statement for the food industry which declared that "mergers and acquisitions by retail food chains which result in combined annual food store sales in excess of $500 million annually raise sufficient questions . . . to warrant attention and consideration by the Commission. . . ."[31]

The FTC and court are not just concerned with mergers among firms with significant market share. They also have ruled in cases against mergers in fairly concentrated industries but involving the elimination of relatively insignificant shares of the market. For example, in Alcoa-Rome, a merger between Aluminum Company of America and Rome Cable Corporation,

---

[31]"FTC Merger Guidelines: Stemming the Tide," *Columbia Journal of Law and Social Problems,* Vol. 5, No. 2 (August 1969), p. 142.

the court said that if a large company in an industry acquires a relatively small company, the merger may be unlawful—even if the merger only adds 1.3 percent market share to the larger company.[32]

Although the court's primary position has been against mergers involving additional concentration of oligopolistic markets even if the additional concentration is small, there have also been decisions favorable to companies attempting to merge in fragmented industries. The landmark case which delineated the thinking of the court with respect to mergers in fragmented industries was *Brown Shoe v. U.S.*[33] A merger was effected between Brown Shoe Company, the third largest shoe retailer, and G. R. Kinney Corporation, the eighth largest shoe retailer. Although the merger had vertical implications, the court was primarily concerned with the horizontal effects since the merger created the nation's second largest shoe retailer. In addition to being the second largest shoe retailer, women's shoe sales exceeded 20 percent of market share in 32 cities; children's shoe sales exceeded 20 percent in 31 cities and 40 percent in 6 cities. Brown and Kinney's combined market share, however, exceeded only 5 percent in 47 cities.[34]

Since there were no quantitative or qualitative measures to determine objectively if competition was substantially lessened, the merger had to be analyzed relative to its economic or social functions within the industry. What trends are occurring in the industry? Concentration or fragmentation? Will barriers to entry for suppliers and/or buyers be realized by the merger? Concern also seemed primarily to rest on the effect of the merger on future merger attempts. Although the combined shares of Brown's and Kinney's markets constituted approximately 5 percent, "if a merger achieving 5 percent control were now approved, we might be required to approve future merger efforts by Brown's competitors seeking similar market shares."

Similarly, in *U.S. v. Von's Grocery Company* the court affirmed the Government's attempt to force divestiture of a merger between Von's Grocery Chain, the third largest retail grocery chain in Los Angeles, and Shopping Bag Food Stores, the sixth largest retail grocery chain.[35] The resulting merged company subsequently became the second largest retail grocery chain in Los Angeles. Not only had Von's and Shopping Bag's penetration of the market increased substantially for a decade prior to the 1960 merger, but there had also been a significant trend toward chain

[32]*U.S. v. Aluminum Company of America,* 377 U.S. 271 (1964).

[33]*Brown Shoe v. U.S.,* 370 U.S. 294 (1962).

[34]The court defined the geographical market to be cities of over 10,000 population in which both Brown and Kinney sold.

[35]*United States v. Von's Grocery Co.,* 384 U.S. 270 (1966).

operations during the same period (i.e., number of chains increased from 96 to 150). Since the number of small, independent grocery stores being absorbed through mergers was increasing continually and the trend was toward concentration, the court indicated that "the facts of this case present exactly the threatening trend toward concentration which Congress wanted to halt."[36]

The result of Brown Shoe and Von's Grocery was to alert merging companies that mergers involving only 5 percent and 7.5 percent share of the market, respectively, may be considered by the court to be unlawful. The significant consideration in such cases is the trend toward concentration in the relevant market, even if (1) trends toward monopoly or oligopoly are not involved and (2) the effect of the merger on competition is inadequately determined. In other words, rather than applying rule of reason considerations in such cases, the court is simply using factual data (i.e., reduction in the number of single unit stores and increase in the number of chains) to find the mergers illegal *per se*—an approach which is certainly contrary to the intent of Section 7 of the Clayton Act as amended by the Celler-Kefauver Act.

One method for effecting a larger merger which may substantially lessen competition is to utilize the failing company doctrine as delineated in the International Shoe Company case in 1930.[37] Generally, the failing company doctrine suggests that companies may be allowed to merge if one of the companies is in danger of going out of business.

Recently, LTV Corporation was allowed to acquire Lykes Steel, which controls Youngstown Sheet and Tube Company, even though LTV owns Jones and Laughlin Steel Company. The merger would create the fourth-largest steel company and would eliminate competition between Youngstown and Jones and Laughlin but was allowed because Lykes would fail without the merger. There is also speculation that utilization of the failing company doctrine may become more widespread since the courts will disallow most requests for larger mergers.[38]

However, the courts will be cautious to insure that the failing company doctrine and not market control is the primary reason for the merger.[39] As indicated in *Citizens Publishing Co. v. U.S.*, the failing company doctrine can only be applied when "the resources of one company were so depleted and the prospect of rehabilitation so remote that it faced grave probability of

[36]*United States v. Von's Grocery Co.,* Ibid.

[37]*International Shoe Co. v. FTC,* 280 U.S. 291 (1930).

[38]David Ignatius, "Rise in Use of Failing Company Doctrine For Mergers is Seen by Antitrust Official," *Wall Street Journal,* Vol. 61, No. 123 (June 26, 1978), p. 24.

[39]Reichold Chemicals, Inc., *Journal of Marketing* Vol. 42 (Apr. 1978) p. 112.

a business failure." Also, there can be no other alternative purchasers of the failing company.[40]

Relevant Market

A vitally important and difficult procedure in assessing the feasibility of a merger is to define both the geographic and product markets for the merging organization. Identification of these markets is mandatory before the effect of the merger on competition in the market can be established.

In the Brown Shoe Case the court contended that for any given case there may be submarkets as well as product markets. The relevant broad markets are determined by "the reasonable interchangeability of use or the cross-elasticity of demand between the product itself and substitutes for it."[41] In other words, the relevant market should include products identical to those of the merging firm and all substitute or potential substitute products as a result of price changes. For example, in the Continental Can case the court suggested that the relevant product market include both metal and glass container companies because of the significant inter-industry competition between the two types of containers.[42] The identification of these broad markets precludes merging companies from arguing that the merger will not lessen competition between the two companies because they are not competing for the same market—a popular argument for companies with products that are not identical but have similar uses.

Another popular argument among merging companies is that the market is extremely broad, including many competitors and geographical areas in order to establish that the effect of the merger on competition is negligible. In Brown Shoe the court vetoed this argument by identifying submarkets within the broader market where competition could also be restricted. The boundaries of these submarkets are determined by examining the following indicia:

(1) industry or public recognition of the submarket as a separate economic entity
(2) the product's peculiar characteristics and uses
(3) unique production facilities
(4) distinct customers
(5) distinct prices
(6) sensitivity to price changes
(7) specialized vendors.

[40]*Citizens Publishing Co. v. United States,* 394 U.S. 131 (1964).
[41]*Brown Shoe Co. v. U.S.,* 370 U.S. 294 (1964).
[42]*U.S. v. Continental Can Co.,* 378 U.S. 441 (1964).

Although the court identified the procedure for identifying submarkets, subsequent cases suggest that consistent analysis of the indicia cannot be relied upon. For example, in Alcoa-Rome the court indicated that copper wire and cable and aluminum wire and cable were separate submarkets, even though, as the District Court suggested, the two types of conductors require similar production processes, have similar uses and characteristics, and are sold to the same types of customers.[43] The District Court also considered the difference in prices between the two types of conductors and found "that this price difference did not foreclose actual competition." The significance of the market identification portion of the case is that if the submarket included both copper and aluminum conductors, an insignificant amount of competition would be restrained and the merger would have been allowed. However, since the Supreme Court indicated that the conductors were not part of the same submarket (despite contrary evidence), enough competition would be restrained to reject the merger.[44]

In addition to identifying the relevant product market, the court must also identify the relevant geographic market. Section 7 of the Clayton Act indicates that if competition is lessened "in any section of the country," the merger is illegal. In Brown Shoe the relevant geographic market was every city with a population of at least 10,000 in which Brown and Kinney sold shoes.[45] In Alcoa-Rome the entire United States was the relevant geographic market, and in the Phillipsburg National Bank case the market was an area with a population of 88,500.[46] As indicated in *U.S. v. Philadelphia Bank*,[47] the relevant geographic market "is not where the parties to the merger do business or even where they compete, but where, within the area of competitive overlap, the effect of the merger on competition will be direct and immediate."[48]

Conglomerate Merger

While vertical and horizontal mergers involve the acquisition of companies in the same industries, conglomerate mergers consist of the joining of

---

[43]*U.S. v. Aluminum Co. of America,* 377 U.S. 271 (1964).

[44]See preceding discussion of Continental Can where metal and glass containers were in the same market.

[45]*Brown Shoe Co. v. U.S.,* 370 U.S. 294 (1964).

[46]*United States v. Phillipsburg National Bank and Trust Company,* 399 U.S. 350 (1970).

[47]*United States v. Philadelphia National Bank,* 374 U.S. 321 (1963); also *CCH Trade Cases,* 73,245, (1970).

[48]See: Kenneth G. Elzinga and Thomas F. Hogarty, "The Problem of Geographic Market Delineation in Antimerger Suits," *Antitrust Bulletin,* Vol. 18 (1973), pp. 45-80, for a discussion of economic considerations in market delineation.

companies which sell in separate markets. Specifically, conglomerate mergers may involve (1) the acquisition of a nonrelated company selling in noncomplementary markets, (2) the acquisition of a company which sells complementary products (i.e., product extension), and (3) the acquisition of a company which sells the same products in different geographical areas than the merging company (i.e., market extension). From a legal perspective, the significant fact about conglomerate mergers is that there is no direct elimination of competition between the merging firms because the companies sell to separate markets.

Conglomerate mergers are attractive growth alternatives for several reasons. First, since the Government is reluctant to allow vertical and horizontal mergers because of their perceived negative impact on competition, companies that desire to expand through merger have a higher probability of success in terms of governmental acceptance with the conglomerate type merger. With the rise in conglomerate mergers during the last decade, however, the Justice Department is considering the possibility of developing legislation that would ban all large mergers.[49] Second, conglomerate mergers give companies with an abundance of products in the maturity and decline stages of the life cycle the opportunity to penetrate new growth-oriented markets. Third, they allow companies to spread managerial and labor costs and expertise over more products and markets. Finally, conglomerate mergers are often an attractive solution for companies which experience significant seasonal sales fluctuations. For example, if a company experiences sales peaks in the fall and spring, it may acquire a company with products that realize peak sales during winter and summer.

In deciding conglomerate merger cases, the courts have relied on several considerations:

(1) The competitive effect and the effect on barriers to entry by allowing a larger company to utilize its abundant resources to aid the competitive situation of a smaller company.

(2) The elimination of a potential competitor. In other words, after a merger the acquiring firm has no reason to develop products which would compete with the acquired firm's products.

The most significant case delineating the thinking of the court with respect to conglomerate mergers was *FTC v. Proctor and Gamble*.[50] In 1957 Proctor and Gamble, a manufacturer of soaps, detergents, and cleaners, acquired Clorox, the leading manufacturer of bleach. Clorox controlled

---

[49]David Ignatius, "Recent Increase in Conglomerate Mergers," *Wall Street Journal*, Vol. 62, No. 19 (July 28, 1978). "The number of acquisitions of manufacturing and mining concerns with assets exceeding $10 million rose to 96 in 1977 from a low of 59 in 1971."

[50]*FTC v. Proctor and Gamble*, 386 U.S. 368 (1967).

approximately 49 percent of the bleach market, Purex controlled 16 percent of the market, the 6 largest firms accounted for 80 percent of national sales, and the remaining 200 firms accounted for 20 percent of sales.

At the time of the merger, Proctor and Gamble was the nation's largest advertiser and realized substantial discounts from the media. Because of the potential advertising savings and the strong correlation between market penetration and amount spent on advertising, the court felt that the merger would give Clorox additional leverage in the bleach industry with respect to advertising. In addition to the advertising advantage given Clorox, the merger also raised significiant barriers to entry into the market. Not only would potential entrants be reluctant to compete in a market dominated by Proctor and Gamble, but smaller, existing firms would also be more cautious about competing because of "their fear of retaliation by Proctor."

The merger was also attacked on the grounds that it would eliminate Proctor and Gamble as a potential competitor of Clorox. The court suggested that entry into the bleach market through internal expansion would be preferred to entering the market by way of a merger. According to the court, even if Proctor and Gamble did not intend to manufacture its own brand, its presence as a potential entrant would encourage existing companies to keep prices relatively low to discourage Proctor from entering the market.

Like Proctor and Gamble, the court also denied a product extension merger between General Foods and S.O.S. because the competitive advantage given to S.O.S. would present significant barriers to entry.[51] The decision also confirmed that the court would not allow product extension mergers involving a financially powerful firm in an oligopolistic market, especially if the acquiring firm is a potential entrant into the market.

The courts have, however, indicated that a large firm such as Proctor and Gamble can enter a concentrated market if it acquires a small firm which is capable of becoming a viable competitor with the financial and marketing aid of the acquiring firm. When a large firm purchases a small company in order to make the firm a major competitor in a market, the merger is referred to as a "toehold" merger and the acquired company is a "toehold" firm.[52]

The legality of "toehold" mergers was stated in *FTC v. Bendix.* Bendix attempted to enter the replacement market for oil, air, and fuel filters by acquiring Fram, the third leading producer of automotive filters. The FTC indicated that "it made a crucial difference whether Bendix merged with

---

[51]*General Foods Corporation v. FTC,* 386 F. 2d 936 (3rd Cir. 1967); cert. denied, 391 U.S. 919 (1968).

[52]See: *Kennecott Copper Corporation v. FTC,* 467 F. 2d 67 (10th Cir. 1972); cert. denied, 94 S. Ct. 1617 (1974).

Fram or another leading firm, or with any one of the various smaller and less established firms . . ." and that "Bendix was a likely potential entrant into the market which could have come into it through a toehold acquisition."[53]

Joint Venture

A joint venture is an association of two or more corporations that pool resources in order to satisfy the individual business objectives. Competitors enter into most ventures to develop markets which are being inadequately cultivated by existing companies. Specifically, the joint venture may be utilized to develop new products, exploit new markets, or provide research support, source of supply, fabrication activities, or distribution assistance.[54] In fact, ventures serve the same functions and are subject to the same strengths and limitations as mergers. The only difference is that the firms remain independent; therefore, direct competition between the participants is not eliminated.

Although there are numerous cases involving joint ventures, the court's position with respect to the association is delineated in the Penn-Olin decision.[55] The court indicated that joint ventures are subject to regulation according to Section 7 of the Clayton Act and, therefore, may be restricted if competition may be potentially lessened. Prior to Penn-Olin the court relied on the Sherman Act, which forced the Government to prove that competition was restrained or that the associated organizations intended to restrain trade.

In the Penn-Olin case, Pennsalt Chemical Company, (a West Coast producer of sodium chlorate) and Olin Mathieson Chemical Corporation (a user but not a producer of sodium chlorate) merged to produce and market sodium chlorate in the Southeast. When the venture was formed, two companies—Hooker Chemical and American Potash—controlled approximately 90 percent of the Southeastern market. The District Court reasoned that the addition of another competitor would stimulate, not reduce (as was suggested by the Government), competition. The Supreme Court subsequently remanded the case back to the District Court, indicating that the lower court should determine if there were a reasonable probability that the companies would have entered the Southeastern market in spite of the joint venture. The Supreme Court also suggested that the District Court consider

[53]*FTC v. The Bendix Corp., et. al.,* Trade Reg. Rep. 19,619 (1970).

[54]Patrick J. Smith, "Joint Ventures and Public Policy," *Ohio State Law Review,* Vol. 26, No. 3 (Summer 1965), pp. 439-440.

[55]*United States v. Penn-Olin Chemical Company,* 378 U.S. 158 (1964).

whether one of the two firms would have entered the market alone, leaving the other firm on the edge of the market. In other words, as indicated in decisions regarding conglomerate mergers, if there is a probability that one firm will enter a market alone while the other firm remains a threat to enter the market, a venture between the two is unlawful.[56]

Although there is still some question about the legality of joint ventures, the court's review of Penn-Olin would suggest that the court will apply criteria similar to that considered in vertical, horizontal, and conglomerate merger cases.

Vertical Division of Markets

A vertical agreement to divide markets is one in which the manufacturer gives dealers or distributors the exclusive right to sell in a specified territory.[57] There are several reasons for the development of exclusive territories. First, retailers or wholesalers will oftentimes not handle the product unless an exclusive territory is granted. For example, automobile dealers will be unwilling to invest in facilities, parts, large inventories, and service personnel unless an exclusive territory is granted. Second, manufacturers can realize better control over sales and distribution activities. The middleman will be more likely to cooperate by implementing the manufacturer's promotional ideas since there is little chance of competition from middlemen promoting the same brand.

The legal aspects of vertical territorial restrictions are somewhat uncertain as indicated by several rulings of the courts since 1960. One of the cases involved White Motor Company, which required that its dealers sell White's products (trucks) only in specified geographical territories.[58] The District Court found that the activity was a *per se* violation of the Sherman Act because, in essence, White Motor Company was vertically dividing the market among dealers. The Supreme Court received the case and distinguished between vertical and horizontal agreements to divide markets. A vertical agreement is one in which the manufacturer gives dealers exclusive

[56]On remand, the District Court found no evidence to suggest there was a reasonable probability that either firm would enter the market independently. They therefore upheld the joint venture. *U.S. v. Penn-Olin Chemical Co.*, 246 F. Supp. 917 (Dist. Ct. Del. 1965). The Supreme Court affirmed the decision by a divided court. 389 U.S. 308 (1967).

[57]A vertical division of markets is also referred to as an exclusive territorial arrangement, an exclusive distributorship (if done with a wholesaler), an exclusive dealership (if done with a retailer), or a territorial restriction (if the middleman is required to sell only within the designated territory).

[58]*The White Motor Company v. U.S.*, 372 U.S. 253 (1963).

right to sell in a specified territory. A horizontal agreement involves the dealers getting together and dividing the markets among themselves. Although horizontal agreements are illegal *per se*, the court found that too little is known about the economic effects of vertical agreements to make "a summary judgment." Therefore, the result of the case was to condemn exclusive territorial arrangements only if they restrained competition substantially.

Another case that is helpful in explaining the legal aspects of exclusive agency agreements is *U.S. v. Arnold, Schwinn & Co.*[59] Schwinn manufactures bicycle parts and accessories, then distributes the finished product by three methods: (1) through distributors, (2) directly to retailers on consignment, and (3) directly to retail dealers. Schwinn assigns specific territories to its distributors and instructs them to sell only to franchised accounts. Also, the franchised accounts must be in the distributor's territory. The Supreme Court found that requiring the distributors to sell only to franchised dealers was a *per se* illegal restraint of trade and in violation of Section 1 of the Sherman Act.

In order to control distribution territories, Schwinn must, therefore, either only sell on consignment or vertically integrate. According to the Schwinn decision, if title passes to a middleman it is a *per se* violation to restrict territories. The only exceptions to this rule would be if reasonable restrictions were imposed by (1) a failing company or (2) a newcomer to a market.[60] Also, if title does not pass to the middleman (as with manufacturer's agents), the manufacturer can restrict territories.

In 1977, the *per se* ruling in the Schwinn case was overruled by the GTE Sylvania case. In this landmark decision, the Supreme Court ruled that the rule of reason must be applied to territorial restrictions to determine the extent of competition restrained by the distribution program.

Sylvania developed a network of independent franchises to sell Sylvania products in a restricted territory (i.e., franchisees were restricted from establishing outlets at other locations).[61] One of Sylvania's more successful dealers, Continental T.V., was somewhat dissatisfied with Sylvania's distribution practices. After several confrontations, Continental indicated that it was going to sell Sylvania products at another location. Sylvania subsequently responded to Continental by terminating their franchise agreement.

One of the key factors in the GTE Sylvania decision involved interbrand

---

[59]*U.S. v. Arnold, Schwinn & Company,* 388 U.S. 365 (1967).

[60]James R. Burley, "Territorial Restriction in Distribution Systems: Current Legal Developments," *Journal of Marketing,* Vol. 39, No. 4 (October 1975), p. 52.

[61]The restriction of location mobility and restriction of customer selections are considered the same for antitrust purposes.

and intrabrand competition.[62] One of the manufacturer's purposes of developing exclusive territories is to strengthen interbrand competition—competition between manufacturers of the same generic product—by restricting intrabrand competition, competition between dealers of one manufacturer's brand. Marketers have long been aware that restricting intrabrand competition can make the exclusive dealer more committed to the sale of the manufacturer's product. The courts have never accepted the organizational benefits which can be realized by sacrificing intrabrand competition for interbrand competition. They simply consider them together as "competition." In the GTE Sylvania decision, however, intrabrand and interbrand competition were considered separately and the net effect was calculated.

Horizontal Market Division

Horizontal agreements to divide markets have been consistently considered illegal *per se* since the 1890's.[63] Horizontal divisions involve situations where two or more companies on the same level of distribution conspire to allocate geographic territories or product markets. For example, Topco, a cooperative association of retail grocers, violated the Sherman Act by allocating territories for Topco branded products. Specifically, each member of the cooperative was issued a license to sell in a specified territory. Since a member was allowed to sell Topco branded products only within the territorial limits of the license, expansion into competitors' territories was not permitted; hence, a contract in restraint of trade.

The court's opinion of horizontal market divisions was reiterated in Topco:

> One of the classic examples of a per se violation of Section 1 is an agreement between competitors at the same level of the market structure to allocate territories in order to minimize competition . . . the court has reiterated time and time again that horizontal territorial limitations . . . are naked restraints of trade with no purpose except stifling of competition.[64]

Summary

Distribution channel strategies have received much attention from marketers as well as the Federal Government. Early in the development of

---

[62]*Continental T.V., Inc., et. al., v. GTE Sylvania, Inc., Journal of Marketing,* Vol. 42, No. 1 (January 1978), pp. 52-53.

[63]*United States v. Addyston Pipe and Steel Co.,* 175 U.S. 211 (1899).

[64]*United States v. Topco Associates, Inc.* 405 U.S. 596 (1972).

corporations, marketers observed that significant economies could be realized by joining with other channel members and collectively establishing business strategy. Recognizing potential negative effects on competition from such behavior, the Government enacted various statutes designed to curb these vertical and horizontal trade restraints. Specifically, Congress passed the Clayton Act which, as amended by the Celler-Kefauver Act, made exclusive dealing contracts, tying contracts, requirements contracts, reciprocity, acquisition of stock or assets of another company, and joint ventures illegal where the effect of such activity might substantially lessen competition or tend to create a monopoly. In addition, the Sherman Act has been applied by the Justice Department to declare horizontal division of markets to be illegal, *per se.*

Although legislation relative to channel activity is somewhat ambiguous, Supreme Court decisions have specifically identified the legality of most activities. For example, exclusive dealing contracts have normally been declared illegal if (1) the manufacturer's sales volume represents a substantial percent of the total sales volume for a product class or (2) the dealer has a dominant position in the affected market. Tying contracts are always illegal if the seller uses a patented product as the tying product. Reciprocity is illegal if a firm utilizes its market strength to coerce companies into compliance with the reciprocal agreement. Finally, mergers are illegal if there is a reasonable probability that competition will be injured.

Discussion Questions

1. Should large firms be allowed to merge under the "failing company" doctrine even if the merger will result in greater concentration of the industry? Why or why not?

2. The Clayton Act indicates that merging is illegal where the effect may be to substantially lessen competition or tend to create a monopoly. Should the merger between Brown Shoe and Kinney have been disallowed when the language of the Clayton Act is strictly applied?

3. What impact does a territorial restriction have on the seller and distributors? Should territorial restrictions be allowed?

4. What procedure should be followed by Federal Agencies when assessing the legality of joint ventures? Is there ever justification for such collaborative activity?

5. What are the economic effects of reciprocal dealing contracts? Can such an arrangement be justified by analyzing economic benefits and costs?

6. Assess the legality of the following arrangement: A company in the newly formed cable TV industry ties purchase of its equipment to the purchase of a service contract.

7. In what way(s) is the law relative to mergers inconsistent with other antitrust laws? Given the contradictory application of law, how can mergers be justified (other than the "failing company" justification)?

3 PRICING RESTRAINTS: PRICE FIXING

Assigning prices to products is a significant marketing activity because the assigned prices represent the value of the respective products as envisioned by the seller. In addition to representing product value, price is also significant because it is, theoretically, an important variable affecting the relationship between supply and demand. In fact, price is the primary mechanism which can be utilized by companies to bring supply and demand into equilibrium.

Although price is theoretically a function of supply, demand, and market situation (i.e., pure competition, pure monopoly, monopolistic competition, and oligopoly), it can also be affected by (1) the size and financial position of the firm, (2) consumer perceptions of product quality or uniqueness, (3) actual product uniqueness, (4) consumer susceptibility to psychological prices, (5) stage in the product life cycle, (6) the extent to which pricing decisions are decentralized, (7) the buyer's bargaining position, (8) the geographical location of the buyer and seller, and (9) governmental policy.

In addition, prices often reflect unique objectives to be accomplished by a particular pricing strategy. For example, firms may want to achieve market share dominance for a new product, realize a stated return on investment, maintain the status quo, or achieve an average markup for a line of products. Pricing may also eliminate competitors in a particular geographic area, build goodwill with certain favored middlemen, or restrict the full functioning of the competitive system. This chapter examines many of these pricing objectives and identifies specific objectives which are inconsistent with the rules of free enterprise and the rules established by the Federal Government.

Price Fixing

As indicated in Chapter 1, Section 1 of the Sherman Act declared every contract, combination, or conspiracy in restraint of trade to be illegal. This statement of law not only reflects the attitudes of the 19th century consumers and businesspeople toward trusts, pools, and monopolies, but also suggests the direction that they thought the government should take in alleviating these problems. Specifically, proponents of Section 1 wanted to prevent all companies from joining together with the objective of restricting competition and realizing the inherent benefits of monopoly. Rather, they wanted each company to act as one and, therefore, help preserve market characteristics that are consistent with a healthy and viable free enterprise system.

Efforts toward establishment of a philosophical antitrust framework were reaffirmed and delineated in 1897 when 18 railroads conspired to fix prices on all railroad activity west of the Mississippi River.[1]

Relative to this railroad conspiracy, the court indicated that Section 1 should be interpreted literally to mean that every restraint of trade is illegal even if the restraint is reasonable. Reiterating the court's attitude toward restraints, in Addyston Pipe and Steel the court indicated that determining the reasonableness of a contract to fix prices is not an important issue because "we do not think that at common law there is any question of reasonableness open to the courts with reference to such a contract."[2]

In 1911, the Standard Oil case defined a "reasonableness" doctrine known as the "rule of reason" which stated that only restraints which are "unreasonably restrictive of competition" are illegal.[3] Preliminarily, it could be argued that the "rule of reason" gave conspirators a possible defense to a price fixing argument since they could contend that the arrangement was not unreasonably restrictive of competition or that the fixed prices were reasonable. This line of reasoning, however, was struck down in 1927 when bathroom and lavatory fixture manufacturers and distributors were convicted of conspiring to fix prices. According to the court, although the "rule of reason" suggests that only unreasonable restraints are prohibited by the Sherman Act, "it does not follow that agreements to fix or maintain prices are reasonable restraints . . . merely because the prices themselves are reasonable. The aim and result of every price-fixing agreement, if effective, is the elimination of one form of competition . . . ."[4] The court went on to state that even reasonable prices were unlawful because "the reasonable price fixed today may, through economic and business changes, become the unreasonable price of tomorrow."

[1]*U.S. v. Trans-Missouri Freight Association,* 166 U.S. 290 (1897); see, also: *U.S. v. Joint Traffic Assoc.,* 171 U.S. 505 (1898).

[2]*U.S. v. Addyston Pipe and Steel Co.,* 175 U.S. 211 (1899).

[3]*Standard Oil Co. v. U.S.,* 221 U.S. 1 (1911).

[4]*U.S. v. Trenton Potteries Co.,* 273 U.S. 392 (1927).

Although the Court was definite about its position relative to fixing reasonable prices, it left the impression that price fixing may be legal if the conspirators have a relatively small share of the market. In fact, in Trenton Potteries the Court stated that "price-fixing by those *controlling in any substantial manner* a trade or business in interstate commerce is prohibited."[5]

In 1940, however, the idea of market dominance and monopolistic power was abandoned in favor of a ruling that made "any combination which tampers with price structures" unlawful.[6] The case which led to the ruling involved a conspiracy between major and independent oil companies to raise prices indirectly by taking distress merchandise out of deviant marketing channels. Specifically, in the late 1920's a period of oil overproduction caused prices to drop sharply. Eventually the price dropped below production costs, but independent oil companies could not temporarily discontinue producing because they would have lost their customer base. Because of overproduction and since the independents did not have adequate facilities to store their excess gas and oil, they had to find new, non-traditional channels through which they could dispose of the distress product. At the same time, the major oil companies were attempting to develop a solution to reverse the trend toward price wars and eliminate the disposal of gas through deviant channels. In order to accomplish these objectives, each major oil company selected one independent oil company as its "dancing partner" and purchased all the independent's distress oil.

The court found the oil companies' scheme to be a *per se* violation of the Sherman Act "even though the members of the price fixing group were in no position to control the market." Therefore, the court reaffirmed the *per se* illegality of price fixing and also indicated that the effect of the conspirators' efforts on price was immaterial. Prior to 1940, the courts reasoned that combining firms to fix prices gave the conspirators the flexibility, as a monopoly, to raise or lower prices at will. In other words, price fixing was illegal because it gave the conspirators "the power to charge unreasonable prices, had they chosen to do so." In fact, in Sacony-Vacuum the Court of Appeals reversed the District Court's guilty verdict by suggesting that the effect of the scheme on competition and price must be determined. The Supreme Court, however, buried the issue of price and the effect of the conspiracy on price by stating, "For as we have seen, price-fixing combinations which lack Congressional sanction are illegal *per se*; they are not evaluated in terms of their purpose, aim, or effect in the elimination of

---

[5]In *Trenton Potteries,* the conspirators controlled 82 percent of the market.
[6]*U.S. v. Sacony-Vacuum Oil Co.,* 310 U.S. 150 (1940).

so-called competitive ends." Price fixing, therefore, remained illegal *per se*, but the monopolistic impact of the scheme became secondary to the activity itself.

Finally, price fixing agreements may take many forms other than the traditional conspiracy to raise or stabilize prices directly. They may be designed to lower prices, indirectly raise prices by taking distress merchandise out of deviant marketing channels,[7] split markets by rotating bids,[8] maintain prices by distributing price lists to competitors,[9] or fix certain aspects of the price mix by agreeing on mark-ups or discounts.[10] Regardless of the innovations or uniqueness of the scheme, however, all joint efforts to "raise, depress, fix, peg, or stabilize" prices are illegal *per se*.[11]

Vertical Price Fixing and Resale Price Maintenance

Although horizontal price fixing has consistently been considered illegal *per se*, vertical price fixing has assumed a different posture. Prior to 1937, the attitude of the court was the same for vertical and horizontal price fixing. In fact, in *Dr. Miles Medical Company v. John D. Park and Sons Company*,[12] the Supreme Court held that "a series of vertical price agreements between a manufacturer and his several retail distributors tended to stifle competition among retailers and therefore was no more permissible under the Sherman Act than the similar horizontal price fixing agreements."[13] With passage of the Miller-Tydings Act in 1937 and the McGuire-Keogh Fair Trade Enabling Act in 1952, however, vertical price fixing (i.e., resale price maintenance or fair trade) was considered legal in those states which adopted fair trade.[14] In 1975, the Consumer Goods Pricing Act was passed which

---

[7]*U.S. v. Sacony-Vacuum Oil Co.*, 310 U.S. 150 (1940).

[8]*Las Vegas Merchant Plumbers Association v. U.S.*, 210 F. 2d 732 (9th Cir.), cert. denied, 348 U.S. 817 (1954).

[9]*United States v. Utah Pharmaceutical Assoc.*, 371 U.S. 24 (1964).

[10]*California Retail Growers and Merchants Association v. U.S.* 139 F. 2d 978 (9th Cir., 1943), cert. denied, 322 U.S. 729 (1944).

[11]*U.S. v. Sacony-Vacuum*, op. cit.

[12]*Dr. Miles Medical Company v. John D. Park and Sons Company*, 220 U.S. 373 (1911).

[13]John A. Humback, "Fair Trade: The Ideal and Reality," *Ohio State Law Journal*, Vol. 27, No. 1 (Winter 1966), pp. 146-147.

[14]Miller-Tydings Act exempted vertical price fixing arrangements from Federal Laws in Fair Trade States; the McGuire-Keogh Act legalized the non-signer clause.

repealed the Miller-Tydings and McGuire Acts and made vertical price fixing illegal *per se.*

Fair trade legislation was designed to protect small retailers from the price cutting practices of chain stores and discounters. It was also an attempt to protect a manufacturer's brand from being used as a loss leader, thereby maintaining the brand's goodwill. These objectives were accomplished by allowing manufacturers to establish a price below which retailers could not sell. Also, this could be accomplished without the consent of the manufacturer's dealers. The manufacturer had only to get one dealer to accept the price agreement, and all additional dealers that sold the manufacturer's product were automatically bound to the agreement (i.e., the "nonsigner clause").

The result of fair trade was to compromise one of the most fundamental principles of free enterprise: the right of free price. All independent businessmen at every level of distribution should be allowed to price merchandise which they own at a price of their own choosing. The elimination of this right is the first step toward the elimination of free enterprise.

Aside from the philosophical argument condemning resale price maintenance, there are several facts which reveal its effect.

1. It had no effect on reversing the trend toward development of chain stores. Primarily, fair trade protects small retailers from competition rather than protects the manufacturer's brand image.
2. Despite legislation, discounters consistently undersold the fair trade price. Since the manufacturers had to control violation of fair trade laws, regulation was virtually impossible.
3. It gave chains "an excuse to avoid price cutting" during the 1930's when profits were low and costs were high.[15]
4. Fair trade is theoretically impractical for many manufacturers. First, economic theory suggests that price decreases are accompanied by increases in demand. Among many manufacturers, price cutting at retail is encouraged in order to stimulate demand. Second, manufacturers that frequently change product models or styles desire price reductions to sell old models that remain at the end of the model or style period.[16]
5. Prices in fair-trade states where price competition is eliminated were generally higher than in non-fair-trade states.[17]

[15]L. Louise Luchsinger and Patrick M. Dunne, "Fair Trade Laws—How Fair? *Journal of Marketing,* Vol. 42, No. 1 (January 1978), pp. 52-53.

[16]Richard W. Sweat, "Resale Price Maintenance: The Nature and Validity of Fair-Trade Laws," *University of Illinois Law Forum,* Vol. 1967 (Summer 1967), p. 313.

[17]Sweat, "Resale Price Maintenance," pp. 315-316.

Identification of Conditions
Favorable to Price Fixing

In an economic system with thousands of businesses and innumerable distribution channel configurations, relationships, and transactions, the detection of unlawful activities is extremely difficult, time-consuming, and expensive. Because of these detection problems and since the FTC and Justice Department have limited resources with which to pursue price fixing conspiracies, it is necessary that they optimally allocate these resources to businesses and situations where the probability of uncovering anticompetitive and collusive activity is greatest. As indicated by Posner, such an "economic approach" to the detection of price fixing is an effective and economically efficient first step to the subsequent punishment of conspirators.[18]

The first condition which is favorable to price fixing is an oligopolistic market. In an oligopoly there are only a few sellers that dominate a significant proportion of the market. Since each firm in the oligopolistic industry is sensitive to the pricing decisions of its competitors, any attempt to improve sales volume by reducing price will be met by similar price reductions from competitors. Also, since the price reductions have little impact on total demand in the industry (i.e., inelasticity of demand), the firms in the oligopoly simply realize the same output at a lower price, thus reducing profits. In order to alleviate the probability of price cutting and the attendant decline in profits, oligopolists often prefer to cooperate in setting price at a profitable level.

A second, related condition is the "significance of the competitive fringe."[19] In other words, if there are 40 or 50 small fringe sellers that command 20 percent of the market, then their influence may restrict the price fixing activities of the 4 or 5 firms that dominate 80 percent of the market. Not only would it be difficult to organize a group of 50 firms, but the fringe firms may aggressively compete and take market share from the dominant firms.

Another important condition affecting price fixing decisions is the number and closeness of substitute products. If there are numerous, available substitute products, the potential for conspiracy is greatly reduced. If the oligopolist attempts to realize monopolistic profits by collusively fixing prices, buyers will eventually abandon the high-priced item in favor of a substitute. Also, the high profits will encourage other sellers to enter the

---

[18]Richard Posner, *Antitrust Law,* the University of Chicago Press (Chicago, 1976), p. 55.
[19]Phillip Areeda, *Antitrust Analysis,* Second Edition, Little, Brown and Company (Boston, 1974), p. 232.

market, thus increasing competition and reducing the power and control of the oligopolists.

Generally, firms with a high ratio of fixed costs to total costs will be encouraged to fix prices rather than experience significant losses in the event of reductions in demand. In a competitive market, reductions in demand are accompanied by output cuts and price declines. Since such a development (i.e., output cuts and price declines) would be disastrous to a company with relatively high fixed costs, agreeing on non-competitive high prices is an attractive alternative.

A fifth condition favorable to price fixing is the decentralization of pricing decisions. The "decentralization" condition coupled with a sixth condition, rewarding salesmen on the basis of profit, can be a dangerous combination.[20] Of course, these factors alone would not automatically warrant an investigation. But, if the industry is highly competitive, dominated by several large firms, and in the mature stage of its life cycle, pressures to control price and profits are great. Salesmen are pressured to meet quotas and maintain simultaneously a specified profit margin in an industry with declining demand and increasing competition. Since they have these profit-making pressures as well as the flexibility to determine price, it is tempting to conspire with other salesmen to split business without competing on the basis of price.

Another significant condition that should be examined by the regulatory agencies is the history or "culture" of the industry.[21] For example, the paper industry and, in particular, the folding-carton industry have developed a reputation as price fixers. In fact, the cultural norm for price fixing is so strong that company executives will resort to violence to get their colleagues to agree to the conspiracies. For example, at a 1974 meeting of consumer-bag producers at Antoine's Restaurant, the president of Chase Bag Company became enraged at the president of American Bag and Paper Corporation for not effecting an established price increase. The argument became so heated that the president of American Bag invited the other conspirator outside for a fist fight. Observers of this industry have defined the problem as a case of not being able "to teach old dogs new tricks."[22]

Finally, trade association activities can provide an effective channel through which executives can meet to fix prices. Since trade association meetings unite decision makers from competing firms for formal and informal meetings and discussion, the development of price fixing schemes is

---

[20]Jeffrey Sonnenfeld and Paul R. Lawrence, "Why do Companies Succumb to Price Fixing," *Harvard Business Review,* Vol. 56 (July-August 1978), pp. 149-151.

[21]Sonnenfeld and Lawrence, p. 149.

[22]Timothy D. Schellhardt, *Wall Street Journal,* Vol. 61, No. 87 (May 4, 1978), pp. 1, 14.

facilitated. Also, trade associations serve as an effective but often illegal clearing house for the dissemination of information about industry prices. For example, the American Hardwood Manufacturers' Association developed an "open competition plan" which required that each member submit to the association daily sales reports, production schedules, and monthly price lists in order to insure "a certain uniformity of trade practice" and "to keep prices at reasonably stable and normal levels."[23] Although dissemination of company information is not always illegal, it is unlawful if the activity's purpose is to restrict production and maintain prices. In the Hardwood Manufacturers' case the court stated that:

> The "Plan" is, essentially, simply an expansion of the gentlemen's agreement of former days, skillfully devised to evade the law. To call it open competition because the meetings were nominally open to the public, or because some voluminous reports were transmitted to the Department of Justice, or because no specific agreement to restrict trade or fix prices is proved, cannot conceal the fact that the fundamental purpose of the "Plan" was to procure "harmonious" individual action among a large number of naturally competing dealers with respect to volume of production and prices. . . .[24]

Conscious Parallelism

In some cases, an apparent price fixing scheme may be inferred from the parallel actions of several business organizations. This interdependent behavior which appears to be an explicit conspiracy to fix prices is known as "conscious parallelism." For example, several retailers might raise their prices at approximately the same time by the same dollar amount. Although such evidence may oftentimes seem to be conclusive,[25] "the Court has never held that proof of parallel business behavior conclusively establishes agreement."[26] Conscious parallelism of action is pervasive and easy to prove, but such evidence without substantiation will not support a case to "prove" conspiracy.[27] However, it may be used to show that price fixing probably did exist. When such circumstantial evidence (i.e., parallel behavior) suggests that a possible price fixing scheme exists, it then becomes the responsibility

---

[23]*American Column and Lumber Company v. United States,* 257 U.S. 377 (1921).

[24]*American Column and Lumber Company v. United States,* Ibid.

[25]*Interstate Circuit, Inc. v. United States,* 306 U.S. 208 (1939).

[26]*Theatre Enterprises, Inc. v. Paramount Film Distributing Corporation,* 346 U.S. 537 (1954).

[27]*Delaware Valley Marine Supply Co. v. American Tobacco Co.,* 297 F. 2d 199 (3rd Cir 1961), cert. denied, 369 U.S. 839 (1962).

of the defendant to prove that the charges are false and the conspiracy does not exist.[28]

One of the primary reasons conscious parallelism cannot be utilized as conclusive evidence of a conspiracy is that such activities as oligopolistic pricing (i.e., price leadership) would be considered unlawful. An oligopolist's price is significantly affected by the pricing decision of individual competitors. When a firm reduces its price in order to expand output, competitors normally identify the price reduction and respond by meeting or even beating the competitive price. Although the oligopolist's price may, in some cases, resemble a monopolist's price and in fact be higher than a price determined by the purely competitive forces of supply and demand, it is independently determined and logically based on an examination of competitors' decisions and reactions. To rule categorically that price fixing exists whenever parallel behavior (i.e., oligopolistic interdependence) is identified would be to forbid the utilization of competitive information in price-making—a totally impractical and unenforceable law.

With the 1974 amendment, which criminalized price fixing and made it a felony rather than a misdemeanor, the Government's burden of proving a conspiracy may become greater, and the court's tolerance of circumstantial evidence, which was the basis for proving numerous price fixing schemes, may decline. In fact, several retailers allegedly conspired to fix prices for hearing aids which they sold to the state for $180 over cost. The District Court indicated that the Government may be required to prove "specific intent" as well as prove that an "overt act" exists in order to prosecute for felonious price fixing.[29]

Indirectly Controlling Price—Legally

Although overt conspiracies to control price have consistently been declared illegal *per se*, the same result can be realized by refusing to sell to companies that raise or lower price. In vertical price fixing schemes, for example, manufacturers will often violate the law by coercing dealers into maintaining prices. The practice is illegal because of the verbal or written

---

[28]*Carlyle Michelman, Trustee of Textura, Ltd., in Bankruptcy Proceedings, Fenestra Fabrics, Inc., and Malcolm G. Powrie v. Clark-Schwebel Fiber Glass Corp., Burlington Industries, Inc., and J. P. Stevens & Co., Inc.,* "Legal Developments in Marketing," *Journal of Marketing,* Vol. 40, No. 2 (April 1976), p. 87; also, *United States v. Champion International Corp.,* "Legal Developments in Marketing," *Journal of Marketing,* Vol. 40, No. 2 (April 1976), pp. 87-88.

[29]*U.S. v. Nu-Phonics, Inc.,* "Legal Developments in Marketing," *Journal of Marketing,* Vol. 42, No. 2 (April 1978), p. 113.

coercive behavior of the manufacturers. The same manufacturers may, however, eliminate the dealers for discounting merchandise as long as they do not coerce the dealers into raising, lowering, or maintaining prices. For example, Farah Manufacturing has a policy of not dealing with retailers that discount its "in-season" men's clothing. Although Farah's salesmen are forbidden to discuss price with dealers or coerce them into maintaining original mark-ups, they are requested to report any discounting retailers to the home office. Upon learning of the "discounter," Farah will unilaterally and legally terminate relations with the dealer.[30]

Once dealers and distributors become aware of the manufacturer's unwritten and unspoken policy of eliminating "discounters," they will, in many cases, maintain suggested prices. This pricing behavior for vertical arrangements is similar to the horizontal pricing phenomenon, "conscious parallelism"or"oligopolisticinterdependence."Insteadofeliminatingdealers, however, the dominant price leader in an oligopoly will possibly injure or eliminate a price-cutting competitor by meeting the price reduction with more significant price reductions. Although these implied horizontal pricing arrangements involve indirect coercion of competitors rather than dealers, the effect of the arrangements is the same: maintenance or stabilization of price.

Delivered Pricing

Delivered pricing is a system utilized by sellers to maintain the same price to all buyers in a particular area regardless of differences in transportation costs. One type of delivered pricing system, basing-point pricing, was particularly popular among firms that had several manufacturing facilities. Cement manufacturers may, for example, utilize Dallas as a basing point, the point from which all transportation charges are computed regardless of the actual shipping point and shipping costs. Assume that a cement producer also has a plant in Phoenix and sells to a buyer in Tucson. Although the buyer's cement is actually produced and shipped from Phoenix, transportation charges are computed from Dallas to Tucson. The difference between "billed" freight charges (i.e., Dallas to Tucson) and actual freight costs (i.e., Phoenix to Tucson) is called "phantom freight." A situation where all shipping costs are computed from Dallas is called "single-basing point pricing." As the Phoenix regional market develops and competition increases, however, cement companies might develop a "multiple basing-

---

[30]*Garrett's, Inc. v. Farah Manufacturing Company, Inc.*, "Legal Development in Marketing," *Journal of Marketing*, Vol. 40, No. 4 (October 1976), p. 113.

point" system where both Dallas and Phoenix serve as basing points. For customers located in the West, freight charges are computed from Phoenix and for customers located in other areas of the U.S., charges are calculated from Dallas.

The primary problem with a basing-point pricing system is that it promotes price uniformity and, therefore, restricts price competition. The legality of the practice, however, is primarily dependent on the way in which the basing-point system is developed and administered. If competitors conspire to develop a basing-point system, then it is illegal. For example, cement producers agreed to maintain uniform prices by utilizing a basing-point system. The court indicated that the practice was an unlawful method of competition in violation of Section 5 of the Federal Trade Commission Act since the cement producers did engage in a conspiracy to fix rates.[31]

Although the court has consistently indicated that basing-point systems which are jointly determined and agreed upon by competitors are illegal, it h.., not made basing-point pricing illegal *per se*.[32] If companies use a basing-point pricing system without conspiring to make it an industry-wide practice, the legality is still somewhat uncertain. All cases that have reached the Supreme Court have involved evidence of conspiracies. At this time, therefore, the status of the law relative to basing-point pricing is the same as it was in 1949 as envisioned by Senator Kefauver in the following statement:

> I am not advocating the abandonment of independent, noncollusive, non-systematic use of basing points. If any company wants to sell on that basis, it has a perfect right to do so, under the law, today. No one is going to prosecute them, no one is going to complain. There is no Supreme Court case, or decision of any other court in this country, that can be pointed out as prohibiting the independent, nonsystematic use of the basing-point principle. What we do not want to do is to allow producers to get together and conspire, either by actual conspiracy or by systematically using the same prices, in order to defeat competition and create unfair business conditions.[33]

Summary

Price fixing involves a scheme between competitors to raise, lower, or stabilize prices directly through personal interaction or indirectly by (1)

---

[31]*FTC v. Cement Institute,* 333 U.S. 683 (1948).

[32]*Triangle Conduit and Cable Company v. Federal Trade Commission,* 168 F. 2d 175 (7th Cir. 1948), aff'd by equally divided court, 336 vs. 956 (1949); *FTC v. National Lead Co.,* 352 U.S. 419 (1957); *Bond Crown & Cork Co. v. FTC,* 176 F. 2d 974 (1949).

[33]William Simon, *Geographic Pricing Practices,* Callagan and Company (Chicago, 1950), p. 152; from *Congressional Record,* August 11, 1949, p. 11481.

taking distress merchandise out of deviant market channels, (2) rotating bids, (3) distributing price lists to competitors, or (4) agreeing on standard markups or discounts. The court's attitude toward these direct and indirect schemes to fix prices is very clear. They are, under all circumstances, illegal even if the fixed prices are reasonable and even if the conspirators are small and control an insignificant proportion of the market.

In order for the FTC and Justice Department to utilize their resources effectively to identify price fixing schemes, it is important for them to identify industries where the probability of a conspiracy is greatest. In an attempt to identify such industries, the following conditions have been suggested as being most favorable to price fixing schemes: (1) oligopolistic market structure; (2) insignificance of a competitive fringe; (3) small number of close substitutes; (4) firms with a high ratio of fixed costs to total costs; (5) decentralized decision making; (6) industries with a history of price fixing schemes; (7) availability of a trade association.

Discussion Questions

1. Discuss reasons why a company would fix prices.

2. If the owners of 2 service stations that were located across the street from each other, fixed gasoline prices, would the arrangement be a violation of the law? Why?

3. Are the high fines and jail terms which may accompany a price fixing charge justified?

4. Why is there a tendency for price fixing to occur in an oligopolistic market?

5. What are the economic consequences of price fixing in an oligopoly?

4 PRICING RESTRAINTS: DISCRIMINATION IN PRICE

Discrimination among middlemen can assume any of the following forms:
- Seller-initiated price discrimination—the seller grants a price break to favored buyers.
- Buyer-initiated price discrimination—the buyer coerces the seller to give a price break.
- Discriminatory advertising allowances.
- Brokerage discounts given to dummy brokerage houses which are set up by the buyer—the broker is a subsidiary of the buyer, and discounts are passed on to the parent company.

Originally, Section 2 of the Clayton Act was passed to control discrimination which was initiated by a seller in order to eliminate competition. For example, a national manufacturer might lower prices in one market area to run small, local manufacturers out of business while keeping prices high in other parts of the country. Since prices remained high in other geographical areas, the national manufacturer could cover losses realized in the small, local area. The small, local manufacturer, on the other hand, had no market penetration of other geographical markets and, therefore, no means of making up losses. Congress responded to this business practice by passing the Clayton Act which made it "unlawful for any person engaged in commerce . . . to discriminate in price between different purchasers of commodities . . . where the effect of such discrimination may be to substantially lessen competition or tend to create a monopoly in any line of commerce."

The primary problem with the Clayton Act as an instrument for controlling discrimination was that it only alleviated injuries to competition on the primary level of distribution (i.e., between sellers). It did not apply to discriminatory prices which were induced by the buyer and had the effect of injuring competition at the buyer level. For example, chain store A could have coerced manufacturer A into granting it a price which was lower than the price granted to independent store B. If independent store B subsequently could not compete effectively with chain store A because of the price differential, it would possibly go out of business, thus reducing competition. According to the courts, however, the amount of competition reduced was relatively small and did not meet the "substantially lessening competition" requirement of the Clayton Act.[1]

Other loopholes of Section 2 of the Clayton Act included the following: (1) Discounts such as brokerage discounts, advertising allowances, trade discounts, and quantity discounts could arbitrarily be granted to buyers without fear of violating the law. Discriminatory prices could, therefore, be indirectly offered to selected buyers through a discriminatory discount program; (2) An acceptable defense to price discrimination was the meeting or "beating" of the low price of a competitor. Since it was simple to locate a competitor with relatively low prices, a price reduction below the price level of the competitor could, in almost all cases, be justified.

In summary, the nature of distribution channels and channel members changed significantly from 1914 to 1930. The Clayton Act was passed to regulate pricing problems in a free enterprise structure that was dominated by relatively small, independent retailers who purchased from an independent wholesaler. When chain stores appeared in the 1920's, the status quo was disrupted by the introduction of a new channel structure which bypassed the wholesaler. Manufacturers rushed to meet the needs of this attractive and profitable new market by offering special price concessions and meeting the discriminatory discount demands of the chains. In order to control the power of the chains and sustain the existence of small, independent businesses, Congress passed the Robinson-Patman Act, an amendment to Section 2 of the Clayton Act.

Section 2 of the Robinson-Patman Act plugged the loopholes of the Clayton Act, making discriminatory prices, discounts, or allowances at any distribution channel level illegal by specifically delineating the conditions under which price differentials can be offered and by making buyer-induced discriminations illegal. All aspects of the Robinson-Patman Act as it relates to discrimination will be specifically examined in this chapter.

Seller-Initiated Price Discrimination

According to Section 2(a) of the Robinson-Patman Act:

---

[1]Buyer level competition was eventually considered as protected under The Clayton Act in: *George Van Camp and Sons Co. v. American Can Company,* 278 U.S. 245 (1929).

. . . it shall be unlawful for any person engaged in commerce, either directly or indirectly, to discriminate in price between different purchasers of commodities of like grade and quality, where . . . the purchasers . . . are in commerce, . . . and where the effect of such discrimination may be substantially to lessen competition or tend to create a monopoly, . . . or to injure, destroy or prevent competition with any person who either grants or knowingly receives the benefit of such discrimination, or with customers of either of them.

As indicated, seller-initiated price discrimination is illegal if (1) competition is substantially lessened, (2) the result of the discrimination is the tendency toward the creation of a monopoly, or (3) the activity tends to injure, destroy, or prevent competition on the primary, secondary, or tertiary level of distribution. In other words, it can be illegal to sell for a low price to customers of a competitor in order to run the competitor out of business (primary level injury to competition), favor selected buyers in a market to obtain their business (secondary level injury), or favor selected wholesalers that sell to retailers competing with retailers who do not buy from "favored" wholesalers (third level injury).

As indicated in Figure 1, primary level injury involves a situation where seller A sells for a low (discriminatory) price in a market which is served by both seller A and seller B but simultaneously maintains a higher price in

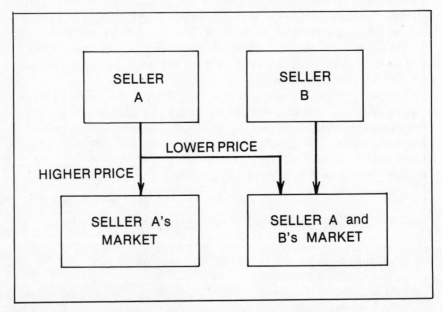

Figure 1: Primary Level Injury to Competition

other markets which are not served by seller B. For example, in 1976 the district court found that Whiteworth, Inc., discriminated in the sale of isopropyl alcohol to customers of Anpak, another drug manufacturer.[2] Whiteworth, the dominant seller of alcohol, sold to customers of Anpak for lower prices than to its other customers. This discriminatory pricing policy forced Anpak either to meet the low prices by selling under its cost or go out of business. The result to Anpak was loss of customers and profits. If the practice were allowed to continue, the result would probably have been loss of a competitor.

Secondary level injury occurs when Seller A grants a price to Buyer A which is lower than the price offered to Buyer A's competitor, Buyer B. Since Buyers A and B are in competition and, therefore, sell to the same customers, it is obvious that Buyer A assumes a competitive advantage with respect to B. For example, Morton Salt Company utilized a "standard quantity discount system" to sell its Blue Label table salt to retail and wholesale customers.[3] The price schedule after deducting discounts ranged from $1.60

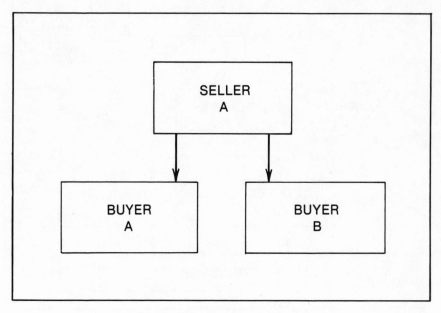

Figure 2: Secondary Level Injury

[2]Anpak Drug, Inc. v. Whiteworth, Inc., review in *Journal of Marketing,* Vol. 41, No. 1 (January 1977), pp. 92-93.

[3]*Federal Trade Commission, v. Morton Salt Co.,* 334 U.S. 37 (1948).

for less-than-carload purchases to \$1.50 for carload purchases to \$1.40 for 5,000-case purchases in any consecutive 12 months and, finally, \$1.35 for 50,000-case purchases in any consecutive 12 months. The Court determined that only 5 companies purchased in substantial volume to receive the \$1.35 price, no independent retailers qualified for the discount, and no known wholesalers qualified. According to the courts, therefore, "theoretically, these discounts are available to all, but functionally they are not." Because the less-than-carload customers were placed at a competitive disadvantage relative to the carload customers, competition may have been substantially lessened.[4]

Third level injury involves injury to the customer of a customer. As indicated in Figure 3, the seller may have two separate channel structures

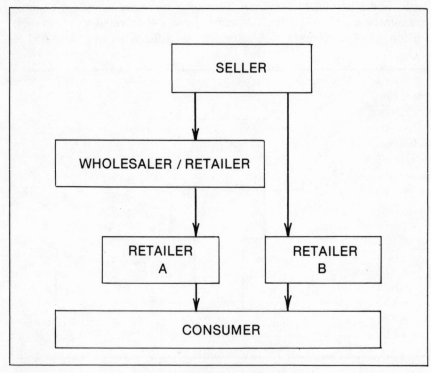

Figure 3: Third Level Injury

[4]Also see: In re Frito-Lay, Inc., *Journal of Marketing,* Vol. 40, No. 3 (July 1976), p. 98. Frito-Lay offered special discounts to multistore retailers by allowing them to aggregate purchases of each unit in the chain.

through which it sells. In the first distribution channel the manufacturer sells to a wholesaler who sells to both retailers and ultimate consumers. In the second channel, the manufacturer sells to a retailer who only sells to consumers. If Retailer B receives a price directly from the manufacturer that is higher than the price received by Retailer A from the wholesaler/retailer, then competition between the two retailers may be lessened. For example, Standard Oil Company sold its gasoline to four jobbers for 1.5¢ below its price to retail service stations in the same geographical area.[5] Although the case involves both secondary and third level injury, the primary focus here is on the third level aspects of the case. Specifically, the jobbers resold to service stations at a price which was below the "tank wagon" price offered by Standard directly to competing service stations. The effect was to reduce competition on the third level of distribution.

Defenses to Price Discrimination

As was indicated in the preceding discussion on seller-initiated price discrimination, price discrimination is only illegal when the effect of the discrimination may be to lessen competition substantially, create a monopoly, or injure competition. The wording of Section 2(a) as well as explicit defenses suggested in 2(a) and 2(b) indicate that companies can offer price differentials under certain circumstances. Specifically, there are seven defenses a company can use in discrimination cases.
- The seller can show that a cost savings was realized from selling to a particular customer.
- The seller is simply meeting the equally low price of a competitor.
- The price differential was caused by normal market/price fluctuations.
- The product being sold at a discount is not of like grade and quality as other products sold.
- The transaction does not involve interstate commerce.
- The buyers are not in competition.
- The item being sold is not a commodity.

Cost Justification

According to Section 2(a), price differentials are acceptable if they are a result of "differences in the cost of manufacture, sale, or delivery resulting from differing methods or quantities." Variations in the cost of selling must

[5]*Standard Oil Co. v. FTC,* 340 U.S. 231 (1951).

be explicitly proven by the seller if cost justification is to be permitted. As evidenced in the Borden Case, the task of proving cost differences can be difficult.[6] Borden gave separate discounts to chains and independents because of the ability to sell in larger quantities to chains and, therefore, realize lower selling costs. The court, however, stated that classification of customers must be based on criteria which is consistent with the considered costs. There are certain independent retailers which are as large as some individual chain stores and, therefore, sell as much milk. These large independents should not be discriminated against simply because they are classified into an ownership category which consists of numerous small independents, thus reducing the average purchase of the group. The point is that categorization for cost justification must be related to the costs being considered and not simply related to something as arbitrary as nature of ownership. This problem is indicative of problems experienced by companies when trying to apply the cost justification defense.

It is also extremely difficult to justify cumulative quantity discount schedules such as the one previously discussed in the Morton Salt Company case.[7] If Company X purchases 12 times per year, for example, the costs of selling and shipping to Company X may be greater than the costs associated with selling and delivering to Company Y, which only orders 2 times per year. If the 2 companies purchase the same quantity of product during that 12 month period, however, both companies will receive the same discount. Also, if Company Y buys a substantially smaller quantity than Company X, then Company Y will probably receive a smaller quantity discount, even though the costs associated with selling to Y are less than sales allocated to Company Y.

Another popular discriminatory practice is to grant noncumulative discounts to firms that order in large quantities. For example, Customer X buys 10,000 units while Customers Y and Z only purchase 5,000 units each. The company grants Customer X a 10 percent discount because of the reduced manufacturing costs associated with producing on a larger scale. Customers Y and Z, however, are as instrumental in reducing the manufacturer's costs as Customer X and therefore should also be given a similar discount. The only time Customer X would be eligible to receive a special discount is when the reduction reflects a cost difference which can be associated with Customer X's buying behavior. For example, if Customer X purchases early enough in the season to help the manufacturer smooth its production schedule and reduce labor needs, it could probably receive a legal discount.

[6]*U.S. v. Borden Company,* 350 U.S. 460 (1962).
[7]*Federal Trade Commission v. Morton Salt Co.,* 334 U.S. 37 (1948).

Meet Equally Low Price of a Competitor

If a company can show that a discriminatory price was offered to meet, in good faith, the equally low price of a competitor, it may be justified by the courts. For example, in the 1930's and 40's, Standard Oil sold gasoline to its jobber customers for 1.5¢ less than the price offered service station customers. The jobbers' gasoline was of the same quality as the stations' gasoline, and both groups were selling in the same competitive area. Also, the jobbers were allowed to sell their gasoline at retail, which placed them in direct competition with the retail service stations for the consumer's business. Since the jobber had a 1.5¢ price advantage, there was price discrimination at the "secondary level."

In a Supreme Court decision involving the facts of this Standard Oil Case, it was noted that substantial precedent has been set to justify the meeting of low price of a competitor if the competitor threatens to deprive a seller of a customer.[8] The 1.5¢ discount was equivalent to the discount offered jobbers by competing oil companies. Although the court did not suggest that the "meeting the price of competitors" proviso was always justification for price differentials, it did indicate that the courts should weigh the injurious effect of a seller's price discrimination upon competition against the beneficial effects of meeting the low price of a competitor.

Although Section 2(b) indicates that a company can offer a price differential to meet the equally low price of a competitor, the courts have restricted its use in some cases. First, a seller can only lower its price to meet the low price of a direct competitor and not to help a customer meet the low price of one of its customer's competitors. For example, Sun Oil gave a Jacksonville, Florida, service station a price reduction so the station could compete with a Super Test Station located across the street.[9] The Supreme Court ruled that since Sun Oil had reduced the price to meet the low price of a customer's competitor and not one of Sun's competitors, the reduction was illegal. Similarly, several oil companies challenged a law in Maryland which forbids oil companies from giving "voluntary allowances" (discounts) to their service stations in order to help the stations meet price cuts of competing stations. The Court of Appeals upheld the law by indicating that sufficient precedent is available to suggest that "the meeting competition defense is only available where the price cut is made to meet . . . the lower price of his own competitor."[10]

Second, the wording of Section(b) indicates that a seller can "meet" the

---

[8]*Standard Oil Co. v. FTC,* 340 U.S. 231 (1951).

[9]*Federal Trade Commission v. Sun Oil Company,* 371 U.S. 505 (1963).

[10]*Governor of the State of Maryland, et. al. v. Exxon Corp., et. al.,* "Legal Developments in Marketing," *Journal of Marketing,* Vol. 41, No. 4 (October 1977), p. 105.

lower price of a competitor, but he cannot "beat" that low price. In other words, a seller can reduce his price to a level which is equivalent to the competitor's price but may not reduce the price below that level. Although this restriction to the "meeting competition" defense seems relatively simple, it can be significantly complicated when the two sellers (i.e., competitors) have products which are not perceived by the consumer as being of the same grade or quality. Specifically, a seller cannot lower the price of a "premium" product to the same price level as a "non-premium" product and justify the reduction through utilization of the "meeting competition" defense. For example, Anheuser-Busch, Inc., selectively lowered beer prices on Budweiser in St. Louis to equal the prices of the non-premium regional beers.[11] The Commission rejected their "meeting competition" defense because the effect of a price reduction of a "premium" product to meet the low price of a "non-premium" product is to undercut the latter product's prices.

Another issue which is closely related to the "beating competition" issue involves the development of new customers when meeting competitive prices. Can sellers use the "meeting competition" defense to penetrate new consumer markets or can it only be used to retain old customer groups? In the Sunshine Biscuit case the Commission ruled that the "meeting competition" defense "is limited . . . to those situations in which a seller is acting in self-defense against competitive price attacks and is not applicable where the seller makes discriminatory price reductions in order to obtain new customers."[12] The Court of Appeals, however, rejected the Commission's reasoning and indicated that Section 2(b) unambiguously states that a seller may lower its price when the reduction is "made in good faith to meet an equally low price of a competitor." They went on to state that the statement does not differentiate between "new" and "old" customers and that the Commission's connotation is unworkable and economically unsound.

Fourth, the seller cannot use the "meeting competition" defense to meet a competitor's price that is unlawful. For example, A. E. Staley Manufacturing Company sold glucose to candy producers for a delivered price (i.e., basing-point price) based on transportation charges from Chicago.[13] Staley attempted to justify the illegal basing-point pricing policy by arguing that they were simply meeting their competitors' basing-point systems. The court's response to Staley's argument was as follows: "We think the conclusion is inadmissable in view of the clear Congressional purpose not to sanction by Section 2(b) the excuse that the person charged with a violation of the law was merely adopting a similarly unlawful practice of another."

---

[11]*Anheuser-Busch, Inc. v. Federal Trade Commission,* 289 F. 2d 835 (7th Cir. 1961).
[12]*Sunshine Biscuits, Inc. v. Federal Trade Commission,* 306 F. 2d 48 (7th Circuit, 1962).
[13]*Federal Trade Commission v. A. E. Staley Manufacturing Company,* 324 U.S. 746 (1945).

Normal Market Price Fluctuations

Section 2(a) states that price changes can be made in response to "changing conditions affecting the market for or marketability of the goods." Some of the stated conditions include (but are not limited to) (1) "deterioration of perishable goods," (2) "obsolescence of seasonal goods," (3) "distress sales under court process," and (4) "sales in good faith in discontinuance of business in the goods concerned."

Commodities That Are Not of Like Grade and Quality

Section 2(a) specifically states that it is unlawful to discriminate between purchasers "of commodities of like grade and quality." If the products are made from different materials or require different production processes, it is legal to offer price differentials. It has been found, however, that products may be considered of like grade or quality even though they are not physically identical. All that needs to be shown, in some cases, is that they are functionally or commercially equivalent.[14] Also, perceived product differences are not enough to satisfy this exemption to the Robinson-Patman Act. As indicated in the Borden case, privately branded milk manufactured by Borden is the same as their nationally branded milk though consumers often perceive privately branded items as being of inferior quality.[15]

Not in Interstate Commerce

There is currently a dual system for evaluating whether a particular case meets the "interstate commerce requirement." On the one hand, the Clayton Act applies only to commerce which is between the various states. In order to regulate price discrimination activities which do not involve interstate commerce, many states have passed and enforced laws similar to the Federal Statutes. Also, if one firm, the injured firm, is not involved in interstate commerce while the firm initiating the anticompetitive activity is an interstate organization, the Federal Antitrust Laws are applicable.

On the other hand, the Sherman and FTC Acts apply to activities which are "in or affecting commerce." For example, Rex Hospital attempted to keep Hospital Building Company from expanding its capacity from 49 to 140 beds.[16] Although the hospital was a local organization, it acquired approximately 80 percent of its drugs and medicines from sources located outside the state's boundaries, and many of the hospital's patients lived in states

---

[14]Louis B. Schwartz, *Free Enterprise and Economic Organization,* The Foundation Press, Inc. (Mineola, New York, 1972), p. 813.

[15]*U.S. v. Borden,* 383 U.S. 637 (1966).

[16]*Hospital Building Company v. Trustees of Rex Hospital,* 96 U.S. 1848 (1976), in "Legal Developments in Marketing," *Journal of Marketing,* Vol. 41, No. 1 (January 1977), p. 90.

other than North Carolina. The court concluded that the facts indicated that
the hospital's activities had a substantial effect on interstate commerce and,
therefore, were subject to federal regulation.

Not in Competition

The only way competition can be lessened by discriminatory activities is
for the recipients of the discrimination to be in competition. If no competition exists, then no injury can be realized. There are several factors which
must be considered in order to establish if competition exists.

    (1) Geographical location of the relevant market—e.g., grocery stores
        in different cities would not share the same market.

    (2) Time of sales—a price given today does not have to be maintained 2
        years from today.

    (3) Level of distribution—a retail sale can be made at a different price
        level than a wholesale sale.[17]

Not a Commodity

The Robinson-Patman Act only applies to transactions which involve
commodities (i.e., products or goods). It does not apply to the pricing
activities of service organizations. For example, pricing of newspaper and
broadcast advertising would not be regulated by the Robinson-Patman Act.
Pricing of services, however, may be regulated as an unfair method of
competition under the FTC Act. Also, the Nonprofit Institutions Amendment to the Robinson-Patman Act "permits nonprofit institutions such as
schools, colleges, universities, public libraries, churches, and hospitals to
receive preferential prices when purchasing supplies for their own use."[18]

Buyer-Initiated Price Discrimination

Commonly known as the "buyer liability" section of the Robinson-
Patman Act, Section 2(f) makes it illegal to induce or receive knowingly a
discrimination in price. This provision was added to the act to keep large
buyers from coercing suppliers into offering them excessively low prices,
an extremely widespread practice in the 1930's.

Although the buyer liability section has not been widely used by the
commission, it was interpreted by the Supreme Court in the precedent

---

[17]Marshall C. Howard, *Legal Aspects of Marketing,* McGraw-Hill Book Company (New
York, 1964), p. 71.

[18]*Abbott Laboratories, et al. v. Portland Retail Druggists Association, Inc., et. al.,* "Legal
Developments in Marketing," *Journal of Marketing* Vol. 40, No. 4 (October 1976), p. 112.

setting Automatic Canteen case.[19] Automatic Canteen Company, a wholesaler of candy and a lessor of vending machines, coerced a manufacturer into giving it prices which were lower than the prices offered to other wholesalers in the same market area. The primary consideration for determining legality of the activity was whether the buyer reasonably should have known that the discount was discriminatory and not based on cost savings. The court ruled that there was no violation of Section 2(f) because of the lack of proof that the buyer knew that the discrimination was illegal and not based on a cost savings.

The Automatic Canteen case placed some significant limitations on the Federal Trade Commission in attacking the recipient of discriminatory prices. First, the commission had to prove that the buyer knew or should have known that the seller was offering a discriminatory price. Second, even if the buyer knew that a discriminatory price was being offered, receipt of the price was legal unless the buyer also knew that no defenses were available to the seller. Third, the buyer had to know that the transaction was significant enough to cause competitive injury.

The problem, of course, with applying Section 2(f) after the court established certain guidelines in American Canteen was primarily in attempting to prove that the buyer should have reasonably known that the price was discriminatory and that no defenses were available to the seller. More recently, however, the courts suggested certain circumstances that would prove buyer awareness without requiring elaborate presentation of evidence. For example, in one case, automotive parts jobbers formed buying cooperatives to receive maximum quantity discounts from manufacturers of automobile replacement parts.[20] Each jobber, however, received its order directly from the manufacturer, thus relieving the cooperative from performing any special services. The court found the individual firms violated Section 2(f) because they "were receiving goods in the same quantities and were served by sellers in the same manner as their competitors, and hence organized themselves into a buying group in order to obtain lower prices than their unorganized competitors." The result of this American Motors Specialties Company case was to indicate that a buyer would be liable of price discrimination if it purchased in the same quantities and utilized similar delivery methods as competing buyers that paid higher prices for the same product.[21]

[19]*Automatic Canteen Company v. Federal Trade Commission,* 106 F. 2d 667 (1939).

[20]*American Motors Specialties Company v. Federal Trade Commission,* 278 F. 2d 225 (2d Cir.), Cert. denied, 364 U.S. 884 (1960).

[21]Also see: *Mid-South Distributors v. FTC,* 346 F. 2d 311 (7th Cir.), Cert. denied, 368 U.S. 838 (1961).

In summary, in order for the Government to prosecute a firm successfully under Section 2(f) it must show that (1) a discrimination in price exists,
(2) the buyer should have known that the price was discriminatory, (3) the
price differential was not justified by one of the seven defenses, (4) the buyer
induced the discriminatory price, and (5) the discrimination was substantial
enough to injure competition.

Finally, there have been several recent developments that may strengthen
the Government's position relative to applying the buyer liability section.
First, in *Kroger Company v. FTC*, Kroger falsely announced to Beatrice
Foods, a supplier of milk and cottage cheese, that it had received lower bids
from Beatrice's competitors.[22] Although Kroger did not actually receive the
"lower" bids, they were still successful in convincing Beatrice that the bids
existed and, therefore, induced them to meet the false bids. In establishing a
"lying buyer" principle, the courts indicated that Kroger was guilty of
inducing a discrimination because it deceived the seller into believing that it
was simply meeting the equally low price of a competitor.[23] Since the seller
believed it was meeting in good faith the low price of a competitor, however,
it was absolved of any liability under 2(a).[24]

Similarly, the FTC recently ruled that A & P induced a discriminatory
price by misrepresenting to Borden that it had received a lower bid on
privately labeled milk and other dairy products. In actuality, however, the
bid offered by Bowman, Borden's competitor, was higher than the bid
offered to A & P by Borden. In confirming the "lying buyer" principle, the
2nd Circuit Court of Appeals indicated that A & P was guilty of inducing an
unlawful price.[25]

Discriminatory Advertising Allowances

Sections (d) and (e) of the Robinson-Patman Act make it unlawful to
make a payment to a customer for services performed by the customer in
selling the product unless payment is made available on proportionally
equal terms to all competing customers. In other words, if an advertising

[22]*Kroger Company v. FTC*, 438 F. 2d 1372 (6th Cir.), Cert. denied, 404 U.S. 871 (1971).

[23]Paul J. Galant: "Buyer Liability for Inducing or Receiving Discriminatory Prices, Terms,
and Promotional Allowances: Caveat Emptor in the 1970's, *Indiana Law Review*, Vol. 7, No. 6
(May 1974), p. 974.

[24]Galant, Ibid.

[25]See: Galant, pp. 978, 979; *The Great Atlantic and Pacific Tea Company v. Federal Trade
Commission*, "Legal Developments in Marketing," *Journal of Marketing*, Vol. 42, No. 4 (October 1978), p. 87.

allowance, display, demonstrator, or any other form of sales device or compensation is offered to one purchaser, a proportionally equal sales device or compensation must be made to all competing purchasers. Elizabeth Arden, for example, offered free demonstrators to about 10 percent of its larger customers and not to the other 90 percent. Many of the outlets which were not given free demonstrators were in competition with the favored 10 percent.[26] The Federal Trade Commission ordered Elizabeth Arden to either eliminate the use of demonstrators or make them available to all competing stores on proportionally equal terms.

Some sellers may design a cooperative advertising program that appears to be available to all competing customers when, in fact, it can only be utilized by a select few of the customers. For example, Hunt Foods, Morton, and General Foods advertised in *Women's Day* magazine, a subsidiary of A & P. Since the magazine was owned by A & P and only sold through A & P's outlets, competitors of A & P had no way of realizing similar benefits from the manufacturers' promotional expenditures. The court stated that the seller is required to make a "frank recognition of the business limitations of each buyer. An offer to make a service available to one, the economic status of whose business renders him unable to accept the offer, is tantamount to no offer at all."[27]

In addition to designing a promotional program that all competing buyers can realistically take advantage of, it is also necessary for the seller to notify all buyers of the program by the same means and through the same channels. For example, if Retailer A receives notice directly from a sales representative of an available promotional plan, then the competing Retailers B, C, and D should also be informed directly by a company representative. In one case, Vanity Fair Paper Mills, Inc., a paper products manufacturer, was asked by a chain retailer to participate in a storewide anniversary sale.[28] Vanity Fair agreed to participate by contributing to a cooperative advertisement. Although Vanity Fair indicated to the commission that they periodically participate in such programs when retailers request their aid, they did nothing to insure that other retailers were aware of this policy. According to the FTC "the seller should take reasonable action, in good faith, to inform all his competing customers of the availability of his promotional program."[29] In Vanity Fair, company representatives did not attempt

[26]*Elizabeth Arden v. Federal Trade Commission,* 156 F. 2d 132 (2nd. Cir. 1946), cert. denied, 331 U.S. 806 (1947).

[27]*State Wholesale Grocers v. Great Atlantic and Pacific Tea Company,* 258 F. 2d 831 (7th Cir., 1958), Cert. denied, 358 U.S. 947 (1959).

[28]*Vanity Fair Paper Mills, Inc. v. Federal Trade Commission,* 311 F. 2d 480 (2nd Cir. 1962).

[29]*Federal Trade Commission Guides for Advertising Allowances and Other Merchandising Payments and Services,* Section 240.8 (1973).

to inform customers of the promotional money that it made available to Weingarten's storewide anniversary sale.

Not only must promotional allowances and services be made available to competing buyers, but they must be made available on "proportionally equal terms." Although the Robinson-Patman Act does not specify the basis for proportionalizing such allowances, the FTC has indicated that it should be fair to all competing customers. The most acceptable basis for allocating funds and services is volume of purchases made by each competing customer. For example, the seller may give each buyer $10 for each case of merchandise sold.

Another important issue that was discussed in *FTC v. Fred Meyer Company* involves seller responsibility when utilizing wholesalers as well as selling directly to retailers. Fred Meyer Company, a chain of 13 supermarkets in the Portland, Oregon, area, received special promotional discounts directly from two suppliers: Tri-Valley Packing Association and Idaho Canning Company. Wholesalers that sold to Fred Meyer's competitors and also purchased from Tri-Valley and Idaho Canning did not receive the allowances which were granted to Meyer.[30] The court confirmed the commission's opinion that Section 2(d) "prohibits a supplier from granting promotional allowances to a direct-buying retailer, such as Meyer, unless the allowances are also made available to wholesalers who purchase from the supplier and resell to the direct-buying retailer's competitors." In addition, the seller must take "reasonable precautions" to insure that the retailers and/or wholesalers are utilizing the promotional funds for their specified purpose.

Finally, as indicated by the wording of Section 2(d) and 2(e), the Government does not have to prove that the discriminatory promotional program has a negative effect on competition. Also, the company that gives the discriminatory advertising allowance may not justify the violation by showing a cost savings. The company may argue, however, that the allowance was given to meet the promotional program of a competitor.[31]

Brokerage Discounts

According to Section 2(c) of the Robinson-Patman Act, only third party, independent brokers can receive a discount for rendering services related to the sale of merchandise. A subsidiary broker of a buyer or seller cannot, therefore, receive a brokerage discount for sales or purchases made through

[30]*FTC v. Fred Meyer Company, Inc.*, 390 U.S. 341 (1968).
[31]See: *Federal Trade Commission v. Simplicity Pattern Co.*, 360 U.S. 55 (1959).

the broker. Also, buyers cannot receive price reductions which are equivalent to the seller's normal brokerage payment for purchasing directly from the seller.

A common practice of chains was to establish "dummy" brokers in order to receive additional price concessions. These "dummy" brokers would normally not perform any brokerage function but would receive payments from the seller for a fictitious service. Payments received by the "dummy" broker would subsequently be passed on to the buyer. The large buyers, such as A & P, argued that the price concessions were justified because of services rendered by the buyer in contracting directly with sellers.[32] Not only has the Court traditionally rejected the application of such a "cost savings" defense to Section 2(c), but it has also rejected utilization of the "meeting competition"[33] and "lack of competitive injury"[34] defenses.

Although the payments and receipt of dummy brokerage allowances and the payment of discounts "in lieu of" brokerage have traditionally been considered illegal *per se*, there have been several relatively recent cases which would indicate that a trend toward reinterpretation of Section 2(c) may have developed. For example, in one case Henry Broch, a food broker, reduced its brokerage charge to Canada Foods Ltd., a processor of apple concentrate, from 5 percent to 3 percent in order to get a 500 gallon order from J. M. Smucker Company.[35] The effect of the discount in brokerage was to reduce the fee charged to Canada Foods and thus allow Canada to meet the price demands of J. M. Smucker. Since Henry Broch was a *bona fide* independent agent, the Court of Appeals indicated that negotiations between Broch and its clients were not covered by Section 2(c). In review of the case, however, the Supreme Court overturned the appellate court's decision. In a 5 to 4 decision, the court indicated that the purpose of the act was to "prevent sellers and sellers' brokers from yielding to the economic pressures of a large buying organization by granting unfair preferences in connection with the sale of goods." Although Henry Broch was an independent broker, he reduced his brokerage to the seller so that the seller could effect the large sale and, therefore, made an "indirect" price concession to the buyer.

According to the dissenting judges as well as numerous observers, the majority's opinion in Henry Broch has the effect of rigidifying brokers'

---

[32]*Great Atlantic and Pacific Tea Company v. Federal Trade Commission,* 106 F. 2d 667 (3rd Cir. 1939).

[33]*FTC v. Washington Fish and Oyster Company,* 271 F. 2d 39 (9th Cir. 1959).

[34]*Great Atlantic and Pacific Tea Company v. Federal Trade Commission,* 106 F. 2d 667 (3rd Cir. 1939).

[35]*FTC v. Henry Broch and Company,* 363 U.S. 166 (1960).

allowances.[36] Also, reductions in the amount of brokerage charged to a seller would be, in essence, a reduction in the seller's cost of doing business and, therefore, justification for granting a lower price to the buyer. In addition to expressing concern toward the court's unwillingness to accept a cost justification defense in cases involving brokerage payments, the dissenters also believed that a seller and a seller's broker should have the flexibility to negotiate brokerage fee. In fact, they suggested that negotiations between a seller and its broker were not even within the scope of Section 2(c).

Although the dissenting judges provided insight into possible weaknesses of Section 2(c) as traditionally interpreted by the court, the traditional approach was not abandoned. The *per se* illegality of discounts "in lieu of" brokerage still prevails, but at the same time discontent with the court's interpretation of 2(c) suggests that reinterpretation or, possibly, Congressional action may be employed in the future.[37] Since the wheels of change in antitrust turn very slowly, it may be several decades before business people are given a logical and consistent interpretation of 2(c) with which to develop channel strategy.

Summary

Discrimination in price may assume several forms and have negative competitive effects at various levels of the distribution channel. A manufacturer might give a lower price to customers in one geographical area in order to run a competitor in that area out of business. On the other hand, the manufacturer might give a lower price to a potential customer simply to get that customer's business. The effect may be to reduce competition between the "favored" customer and other customers that pay higher prices for the same items. Price discrimination may also be accomplished by providing one customer with proportionally higher advertising dollars or support than competing customers. Finally, discriminatory pricing may be accomplished by giving a broker discount to a buyer that performs the broker's function but is not a *bona fide* independent broker.

Price discrimination is regulated by the Robinson-Patman Act which amended Section 2 of the Clayton Act. Specifically, the Robinson-Patman Act makes it unlawful to discriminate in price where the effect of such discrimination may substantially lessen competition or tend to create a monopoly on any level of the distribution channel. The law also requires

---

[36]See: *U.S. Department of Justice Report on the Robinson-Patman Act*, pp. 80-84.
[37]See: *Thomasville Chair Company, v. FTC*, 306 F. 2d 541 (5th Cir. 1962); and *Hruby Distributing Company*, 61 FTC 1437 (1962).

that advertising allowances and promotional support be given on proportionally equal terms to all competing customers. In addition, the Robinson-Patman Act requires that broker discounts only be given to brokers who are independent of both the buyer and seller.

Although price discrimination is illegal where competition is reduced, it is not illegal *per se*. There are, therefore, several conditions which, when present, serve as justification for discriminatory pricing. These defenses are as follows: (1) the seller can show that a cost savings was realized from selling to a particular customer; (2) the seller is meeting the equally low price of a competitor; (3) the price differential was caused by normal market/price fluctuations; (4) the product being sold at a discount is not of like grade and quality as other products that are being sold by the manufacturer; (5) the transaction does not involve interstate commerce; (6) buyers are not in competition; or (7) the item being sold is not a commodity.

Discussion Questions

1. What impact does the Robinson-Patman Act have on price competition?

2. The Robinson-Patman Act not only forbids a seller from granting lower prices but it forbids buyers from inducing price reductions. Should the Government disallow buyers from bargaining for lower prices? Why or why not?

3. Assume that a large, national seller reduces price in the Southwest but maintains higher prices in other areas of the country. A competing manufacturer that only markets its product in the Southwest subsequently feels the pressure of the lower prices and goes out of business. Should the national seller be considered a violator of Section 2(a) of the Robinson-Patman Act for causing primary-level injury?

4. What impact does Section 2(c) of the Robinson-Patman Act (brokerage discounts) have on distribution channel efficiency?

5. Antitrust laws are passed to help stimulate competition and perpetuate free enterprise. Does the Robinson-Patman Act accomplish that objective? Why or why not?

6. What practices which are currently regulated by the Robinson-Patman Act pose a threat to competition? What alternative methods of enforcement could be applied to regulate these practices?

5 UNFAIR AND DECEPTIVE PROMOTIONAL STRATEGY

The FTC Act was originally passed to establish an organization, the FTC, to monitor and take legal action against business practices that were unfair and had a harmful impact on competitors. Concurrent with passage of the act, however, was the rapid expansion and concentration of markets and improvements in transportation and communication systems. Quick to recognize and take advantage of these opportunities, nationally-oriented marketers proliferated and began campaigns to encourage and coerce consumers into purchasing their newly-developed brands. This ultimately resulted in the widespread practice of quackery, the promotion of half-truths and false claims, and the perpetuation of the normative concept of *caveat emptor.*

The common law and the FTC Act were, for the most part, ineffective in attacking these deceptive and devious practices. The common law did not specifically recognize and deal with deceptive advertising, and the FTC's attention was primarily confined to "unfair methods of competition." In 1922, however, the FTC's role as a consumer protection agency was given impetus when the Supreme Court ruled that deceptive advertising was an unfair trade practice within the scope of the FTC's jurisdiction.[1] Although the 1922 ruling suggested that consumer protection was a priority issue, hope for significant change was postponed in 1931 when the FTC's power to adjudicate a case of false advertising was somewhat restricted. Specifically, the Court in *FTC v. Raladam Company* indicated that the FTC was powerless to control false and deceptive advertising unless competition was also injured by the deceptive promotion.[2]

If the decision in *FTC v. Raladam* had any negative effect on the FTC's flexibility to control deceptive advertising, the effect was dispelled in 1938

[1]*FTC v. Winsted Hosiery,* 258 U.S. 483 (1922).
[2]*FTC v. Raladam,* 283 U.S. 643 (1931).

82

with passage of the Wheeler-Lea Amendment. The new FTC Act extended the scope of the FTC by granting it authority to control both "unfair methods of competition" and "deceptive acts and practices." Also, Section 12 of the amended act specifically made it unlawful "for any person, partnership, or corporation to disseminate, or cause to be disseminated, any false advertisement . . . for the purpose of inducing . . . , directly or indirectly, the purchase of food, drugs, devices, or cosmetics." The effect of the Wheeler-Lea Amendment, therefore, was to sanction the FTC as a consumer agency.

Deceptive Acts and Practices

The primary focus of the FTC in promotional matters has been on practices which have the capacity to deceive. Since its inception in 1914, the FTC has observed that deceptive promotional practices may utilize different disguises and assume many forms. Although all deceptive practices have certainly not been revealed, the FTC has, through analysis of numerous cases, indicated to marketers what it will and will not tolerate. Among activities which have been identified as deceptive and, therefore, impermissible are:

- deceptive pricing ("free" goods and "bait" advertising)
- deception by not disclosing important aspects of the product
- using a well-known name as one's own name
- false disparagement of competing products
- false representations of approval or sponsorships (i.e., false endorsements or testimonials)
- deceptive guarantees
- false representations of composition, character, or source
- deceptive demonstrations or mock-ups[3]
- ambiguous statements (each statement may be true but taken as a whole the message has the capacity to deceive)[4]
- implications that the product possesses certain qualities

Criteria for Identifying Deception

An examination of specific cases involving false or deceptive advertising indicates that the FTC has primarily focused on the act of deceiving,

---

[3]Earl W. Kintner, "Federal Trade Commission Regulation of Advertising," *Michigan Law Review,* Vol. 64 (May 1966), pp. 1281-1282.

[4]M. D. Bernacchi, "Substantive False Advertising Standards: Discretion and Misinformation by the FTC," *Journal of Advertising,* Vol. 5, No. 2 (Spring 1976), p. 26.

false statements, and misleading images such as mock-ups and props. Applying this perspective, it becomes apparent that the actual impact of the ad on
consumers is, according to the FTC, less important than the advertisement
itself. In other words, the primary criterion for identifying deception is "the
capacity of the ad to deceive." Showing that consumers were actually
deceived or were damaged as a result of the promotion is unnecessary.

In one case, the FTC attacked a Crisco ad which attempted to show that
frying chicken in Crisco helps eliminate the greasy taste.[5] Specifically, the
actor poured a cup of oil into a skillet and cooked several pieces of chicken.
After the chicken was fried and removed from the skillet, the remaining
mixture was poured back into the cup to show that only one tablespoon had
been absorbed by the chicken, when, in fact, the remaining liquid mixture
was a combination of both oil and chicken fat. The commission indicated
that the ad had the capacity to mislead consumers into believing that foods
fried in Crisco are less greasy than foods fried in other cooking oils. Proving
that the ad did, in actuality, deceive was unnecessary.

Another criterion which has a significant impact on the identification of
deception relates to the type of information evaluated by the FTC in any
particular case. In the Ford Motor Company case the commission stated
that it was not required to look further than the advertisement itself in
interpreting meaning.[6] In other words, studies which showed that consumers
perceived ads differently than the FTC's evaluation of an ad were unnecessary. The Commission could also reject expert testimony in favor of its own
judgment in identifying the reasonableness of an ad.

Consistent with its policy of questioning ads which have the capacity to
deceive, the FTC also strongly considers the ambiguity of ads. According to
the commission, when an advertisement has more than one meaning, one of
which is false, the entire ad can be considered false.[7] In one case, the
National Commission on Egg Nutrition advertised that "there is no scientific
evidence that eating eggs increases the risk of heart disease."[8] Although
some readers may interpret the statement to be an opinion of the NCEN
concerning recent research, others may interpret it as fact. Since one of the
interpretations may be consistent with the alleged misleading aspects of the

[5]Proctor and Gamble, *Trade Regulation Reporter* (January 1972), #19889.
[6]In re Ford Motor Company, "Legal Developments in Marketing," *Journal of Marketing,*
Vol. 41, No. 1 (January 1977), p. 96.
[7]*National Commission on Egg Nutrition and Richard Weiner v. FTC,* "Legal Developments
in Marketing," *Journal of Marketing,* Vol. 42, No. 3 (July 1978), p. 119.
[8]*National Commission of Egg Nutrition and Richard Weiner v. FTC,* Ibid.

ad, the entire message is considered to be misleading.[9] Also, it does not matter how many consumers will read the ad in a misleading way.[10]

TABLE 5-1
Principles for Identifying Deception

• It has the capacity to deceive.

• The FTC does not have to look further than the ad itself in interpreting meaning.

• When an ad has more than one meaning, one of which is false, the entire ad can be considered false.

• It is deceptive to combine statement of facts in such a way as to mislead.

• Deception may be implied as well as explicitly stated.

• If an ad may be read in a deceptive way, even though it generally is not misread, it is illegal.

Reasonable Basis for Making a Claim

Before an affirmative advertising claim can be made about product performance, the advertiser must have a reasonable basis for making the claim. If prior proof of the validity of the claim is unavailable, the advertisement is illegal even if the claim is, in fact, true and the product performs as advertised. According to the commission, "The fundamental unfairness results from imposing on the consumer the unavoidable economic risk that the product may not perform as advertised."[11]

It is unnecessary to use scientific studies to assess product performance and substantiate claims. As was indicated in the Pfizer case, medical literature, knowledge, and clinical experience could provide a reasonable basis for making claims that "UN-BURN" ointment for sunburns "actually anesthetizes nerves in sensitive sunburned skin."[12] Generally, the FTC has suggested that in order to determine the reasonableness of a claim, a case-by-case analysis of the following factors must be conducted:

• type and specificity of the claim made
• type of product
• possible consequences of the false claim

[9]*Ford Motor Company,* op. cit.
[10]*Murray Shoe Corp. v. FTC,* 304 F. 2d 270 (2nd Cir. 1962).
[11]*Pfizer, Inc.,* #20056, FTC Dkt 8819 (July 11, 1972).
[12]Pfizer, Ibid.

- degree of reliance by consumers on the claims
- the type, and accessibility, of evidence adequate to form a reasonable basis for making the particular claims[13]

Effect of Ads on Beliefs and Consumer Research

In addition to focusing on the act of deceiving, false claims and statements, and misleading images such as mock-ups and props, the FTC has recently focused its attention on ads which create or reinforce false beliefs.[14] Applying this perspective, the truthfulness of the actual message is not the most critical issue. What is critical is how members of the audience perceive the ad and how the ad affects their opinions and beliefs about the advertised product or service. In other words, deception would exist when consumer perception of the truthfulness of a claim is inconsistent with the actual truthfulness of the claim.

Although the FTC has recognized the consumer behavior aspects of deception, it still has not operationalized a program of using consumer input as a critical decision variable. Some observers indicate that the FTC's first step in identifying deception should be to test consumer perception of and belief in advertisers' claims. In other words, does the consumer believe in a claim, and is it relevant to brand selection? If the answer is yes and the claim cannot be adequately substantiated by the advertiser, then the ad is deceptive.[15]

In addition to identifying deception which results from erroneous beliefs, other researchers have also identified more subtle deceptions that will definitely not be effectively identified or prosecuted unless the FTC develops a more scientific, behavioral approach. Gardner suggests, for example, that deception can occur because consumers internalize certain beliefs about an ad which are not necessarily true.[16] A detergent manufacturer may find that red and blue crystals in detergent are perceived by consumers as cleaning agents. Even though no statement is made about the relative efficacy of the crystals, consumers believe they are effective in getting clothes clean and, therefore, can be deceived by a statement which simply mentions that the crystals are present.[17]

Cohen also approaches the problem of identifying deception by suggest-

[13]Pfizer, Ibid.

[14]H. Keith Hunt, "Decision Points in FTC Deceptive Advertising Matters," *Journal of Advertising*, Vol. 6, No. 2 (Spring 1977), p. 29.

[15]Gary M. Armstrong and Frederick A. Russ, "Detecting Deception in Advertising," *MSU Business Topics*, (Spring 1975), pp. 21-31.

[16]David M. Gardner, "Deception in Advertising: A Conceptual Approach," *Journal of Marketing*, Vol. 39 (January 1975), p. 42.

[17]Gardner, Ibid.

ing that surrogate indicators may be used to perpetuate deception without explicitly making a false or misleading claim. A surrogate indicator is a "cue actually used by the consumer in place of another to evaluate alternatives."[18] For example price may be used to evaluate quality, or color may be used to evaluate richness of flavor in ice cream.[19] Although the FTC has periodically attacked ads that use certain surrogate indicators to imply that the product is unique, it has not developed a procedure for systematically evaluating the effect of these claims on consumers.

Advertising to Children

Since the late 1960's, one of the most controversial public policy issues has involved advertising which is directed at children. On the one hand, critics of child advertising have suggested that children are unable to differentiate between puffery and honesty or fact and fiction and, therefore, are both psychologically and physically vulnerable to potentially hazardous selling appeals. Because of this potential vulnerability, critics have indicated that strict regulations should be imposed on child advertising. On the other hand, however, advertisers and some legislators point out that there is no objective evidence to support a contention that advertising affects children differently than teenagers or adults. Also, proponents of child marketing suggest that restrictions on advertising to a selected group would be a serious compromise of advertisers' First Amendment freedom of speech.

Despite the lack of empirical evidence to support either groups' arguments, the FTC initiated action in 1978 to promulgate a trade regulation rule for child advertising. In essence, the rule is designed to place restrictions on all televised product advertising directed to audiences composed primarily of young children (i.e., under 8 years old). The rule would also require affirmative disclosure of nutritional value of candy, sweetened cereal, and other pre-sweetened foods that pose significant dental hazards. These requirements and restrictions on advertising of sugared products would be directed at both younger and older children (i.e., 8 to 12 years old). Rationale presented by the FTC staff for proposing such strict guidelines can be summarized in the following statement: "Commercials for sugared products are false, misleading, and deceptive because all make at least the implicit claim that consumption of the product is desirable."[20]

[18]Dorothy Cohen, "Surrogate Indicators and Deception in Advertising," *Journal of Marketing,* Vol. 36 (July 1972), pp. 10-11.

[19]Cohen, Ibid.

[20]"Report by FTC's Staff Recommends Major Strictures on Children's TV Ads," *Advertising Age* (February 27, 1978), p. 93.

In addition to a trade regulation rule that could possibly ban all televised product advertising directed to audiences composed primarily of young children,[21] the FTC will also attempt to alleviate the following unfair advertising practices.

- Advertisements that may tend to induce children to engage in dangerous activity
- Advertisements that use hero figures to sell products to children
- Premium advertising to children[22]

Since 1976, the FTC has focused its attention on eliminating ads which have the tendency or capacity to induce children into engaging in unsafe activity. In one case Benton and Bowles, the creator of the Euell Gibbons ads for Post Grape Nuts, and General Foods agreed to cease advertisements which suggest that certain wild plants are edible.[23] Rationale for issuing the consent order was based on the supposition that such ads may have the capacity to influence children to eat potentially poisonous plants. The FTC also indicated that the advertisements allude to the fact that eating wild plants without parental supervision may be acceptable.

In a more recent case, Mego International was directed to eliminate ads which depict a young girl using an electric appliance near a sink filled with water.[24] Specifically, a young girl was shown washing the hair of Mego's "Cher" doll. After she finished washing the doll's hair her mother entered the room to give her daughter a hair dryer. With the sink still filled with water, the young girl then proceeded to dry the doll's hair with the electric dryer. In ordering Mego to cease the Cher ads, the FTC prohibited them from depicting the use of any product in an unsafe manner.

The FTC's concern for the use of hero characters in child advertising was expressed in an order requiring that Hudson Pharmaceutical Corporation stop using Spider Man and other hero figures to promote children's vitamins.[25] The FTC indicated that such advertising takes advantage of the trust relationship between children and hero figures, induces children to

[21]In re Proposed Trade Regulation Rules for Children's Advertising, "Legal Developments in Marketing," *Journal of Marketing,* Vol. 42, No. 4 (October, 1978), pp. 90-91; and George Hartman, "Move on Ads Aimed at Kids is Ominous," *Marketing News,* Vol. 11, No. 22 (May 5, 1978), p. 3.

[22]Dorothy Cohen, "FTC Adding 'Unfairness' to Illegality as Action Criterion," *Marketing News,* Vol. 11, No. 2 (July 15, 1977), p. 12.

[23]In re Benton & Bowles, Inc., "Legal Developments in Marketing," *Journal of Marketing,* Vol. 41, No. 2 (April 1977), p. 106.

[24]In re Mego International, Inc., "Legal Developments in Marketing," *Journal of Marketing,* Vol. 42, No. 4 (October 1978), p. 91.

[25]In re Hudson Pharmaceutical Corp., "Legal Developments in Marketing," *Journal of Marketing,* Vol. 41, No. 2 (April 1977), p. 105.

take excessive quantities of vitamins, and leads children to believe the product has extraordinary qualities which do not exist.

Premium advertising is an attempt by advertisers to influence children to purchase a product for the accompanying prize, even if the product is undesirable. Although not always deceptive, illegal, or unfair, premium advertising represents a potentially powerful tool for influencing the purchase attitudes and behavior of children. There is also evidence that parents submit to the desire of their children to purchase the product in order to acquire the premium. Parents allegedly rationalize the purchase of a prize by reasoning that "someone in the family would eventually consume the product."[26] On the other hand, although parents rationalize the purchase of a product to acquire a prize, 74.4 percent of parents in a study suggested that premium advertising is overemphasized in ads to the point that product attributes represent secondary purchase appeals.[27]

Comparison Advertising

In narrow terms, comparison advertising involves the comparison of "two or more specifically-named or recognizably-presented brands of the same generic product or service class in terms of one or more specific product or service attributes."[28] One of the more widely publicized comparison ads was "the Pepsi Challenge" in which Coca Cola drinkers were asked to reveal in a blind taste test which drink they preferred. Comparing Pepsi and Coke in terms of taste, the studies revealed that in excess of 50 percent of participating Coke drinkers preferred Pepsi to Coke. In addition to the Pepsi Challenge, numerous other advertisements have also employed utilization of the comparative technique. In fact, one study revealed that approximately 19 percent of advertisements during one week of viewing could broadly be interpreted as comparative (i.e., including ads in which competition was only implied). When Wilkie and Farris's narrow definition was applied, however, only 3.1 percent of the ads were comparative.[29]

Although consumer groups, advertisers, government agencies, and advertising agencies have frequently expressed opinions regarding the

---

[26]Pat L. Burr and Richard M. Burr, "Parental Responses to Child Marketing," *Journal of Advertising Research,* Vol. 17, No. 6 (December 1977), p. 20.

[27]Burr and Burr, Ibid.

[28]William L. Wilkie and Paul W. Farris, "Comparison Advertising: Problems and Potential," *Journal of Marketing,* Vol. 39, No. 4 (October 1975), p. 7.

[29]Stephen W. Brown and Donald W. Jackson, "Comparative Advertising: Examining Its Nature and Frequency," *Journal of Advertising,* Vol. 6 (November 4, 1977), pp. 15-18.

feasibility of comparison advertising, only a few studies have empirically tested actual ad effectiveness.[30] In one such study, Schick claimed that a 16 percent increase in market share for its Fleximatic shaver could be attributed to a highly successful comparison advertising campaign.[31] In another study, the effects of comparison advertising on the attitudes of beer drinkers was experimentally tested in a laboratory environment.[32] Although inconclusive, the study suggests that neither comparison nor non-comparison ads have any significant competitive advantages over each other.[33]

Although the effect of comparison ads on market share, advertiser image, and competitor image is still somewhat uncertain, comparison ads do provide consumers with biased information on the relative efficacy of 2 or more brands and disparage competitive brands either by implication or by direct criticism. These inherent characteristics of comparison advertising have served as the basis for most public policy decisions. Specifically, the FTC has restated its advocacy of the "consumer's right to know" by supporting comparison advertising as a method of disseminating information with which consumers can make decisions.[34] On the other hand, concern with the negative implications of competitive disparagement and unfair utilization of comparative approaches has been reflected in recent FTC decisions, trademark law, state law, common law, and self-regulation policies.

The most enthusiastic attempt at defining legal or ethical guidelines for comparison advertising has come from the American Association of Advertising Agencies and the major television networks. Specifically, the guidelines adopted by these groups include the following: (1) the ad should inform consumers, not discredit competitors; (2) only significant competitors should be named; (3) competition should be fairly and properly identified; (4) the advertising should compare similar properties or ingredients; (5) it should only involve honest comparisons and not be used to simply upgrade by association; (6) testing should be done by an objective, independent testing source; (7) all claims should be supported by the tests; (8) messages should not reflect partial results or insignificant differences; (9) the property being compared should be significant in terms of value or usefulness of the

[30]See: "Comparative Ads in Center Ring at AAAA Meeting," *Broadcasting*, Vol. 90 (May 17, 1976), pp. 42-44.

[31]"Schick, Inc., Teeters on the Razor's Edge," *Business Week*, (May 5, 1975), p. 38.

[32]William L. Shanklin and Gerald L. Schroader, "The Effects of Comparison and Non-comparison Advertisements on Television Viewers," *Pittsburgh Business Review*, Vol. 47, No. 2 (June 1978), p. 5.

[33]Shanklin and Schroader, p. 8.

[34]See: Wilkie and Farris, pp. 8-9.

product to the consumer; and (10) testimonials should reflect only one person's opinion and not be presented as a representative opinion.[35]

With the support of the FTC, guidelines developed by self-policing organizations and television networks primarily emphasize the necessity of fair and accurate reporting of significant comparisons. As firms deviate from this "fairness" standard, the FTC is quick to respond by treating the practice as an unfair method of competition in violation of Section 5 of the FTC Act. In the Matsushita Electric Corporation case, the FTC not only prohibited the offender from misrepresenting test results but also indicated that Matsushita could not refer to tests as evidence of superiority of its video and audio equipment unless (1) the test is appropriately designed to measure effectiveness of characteristics referred to in the ad, (2) test results establish significant comparative superiority, and (3) the test is based upon a "broad sample of the major or well-known competitive brands."[36] Similarly, General Electric has been ordered to prove all advertising claims for TV sets, clothes washers, clothes dryers, ranges, dishwashers, trash compactors, refrigerators, freezers, room air conditioners, or stereophonic equipment.[37] All superiority claims must indicate the specific area and aspect of superiority, must not be contradicted by any additional evidence, must be proven by scientific studies and tests, and must be beneficial to consumers. Finally, in its "Kroger Price Patrol" campaign, Kroger stated that studies of various grocery items indicate that its prices are lower than competitors'. In filing a complaint, the FTC indicated that (1) Kroger failed to disclose that meat, produce, and private brands were not included in the sample, (2) the sampling procedures were not methodologically correct, and (3) study results did not prove that shopping at Kroger, rather than competitors' stores, would result in lower overall expenditures.[38]

In addition to attacking comparative advertising as an unfair method of competition or deceptive practice, it can also be attacked under common law, state law, and trademark law. In order to effect action under common law as libel or disparagement, the advertisement must (1) identify a competitor or competitive brand by name or implication and (2) disparage the

[35]Presented in: Suzanne B. Conlon, "Comparative Advertising: Whatever Happened to "Brand X"? *Chicago Bar Record,* Vol. 57, No. 3 (November-December 1975), p. 119. Also available from the American Association of Advertising Agencies.

[36]In re Matsushita Electric Corporation of America, "Legal Developments in Marketing," *Journal of Marketing,* Vol. 41, No. 4 (October 1977), p. 110.

[37]In re General Electric Company, "Legal Developments in Marketing," *Journal of Marketing,* Vol. 41, No. 4 (October 1977), p. 110.

[38]In re The Kroger Company, "Legal Developments in Marketing," *Journal of Marketing,* Vol. 42, No. 2 (April 1978), p. 117.

competitor or the competitor's product.[39] State law such as the Illinois Uniform Deceptive Trade Practices Act can also be applied to obtain relief for persons damaged by a deceptive trade practice such as false advertising, disparagement, or unfair competition claims.[40] Finally, when a comparative ad misrepresents or misdescribes the advertised products or services, it may be attacked under Section 43(a) of the Lanham Act.[41] Although having little application when both products are not misrepresented, it was successfully used to keep Anacin from making false advertising claims.[42]

Advertising of Professional Services

Given impetus by several Supreme Court decisions affecting the pharmaceutical and legal professions, advertising of professional services and prescription products has become a significant political, economic, and social issue. In *Virginia State Board of Pharmacy v. Virginia Citizens Consumer Council,* the court declared that rules designed to restrict advertising of pharmaceutical drug prices is a violation of the advertiser's constitutional right of free speech.[43] The court went on to suggest that it is in the best interest of consumers and society to allow advertising of standard products such as prescription drugs.[44] Such arguments which delineate the benefits of advertising are numerous and are substantiated by empirical research. In fact, one such study indicated that the average price of prescription drugs was 4 percent higher in restrictive states than in states where no advertising restrictions existed.[45] Extrapolating this price variance to the entire population, consumers could have saved over $400 million on prescription drugs in 1975 if advertising restrictions had not existed.[46]

In addition to permitting the advertising of pharmaceuticals, the Virginia State Board of Pharmacy case also answered a significant question concerning the constitutional rights of advertisers. Prior to 1976, commercial speech

[39]Conlon, op, cit., p. 124.

[40]Conlon, p. 126.

[41]Conlon, p. 123.

[42]J. J. Boddewyn, "Nations Apply Different Laws to Comparison Ads," *Marketing News,* Vol. 12, No. 7 (October 6, 1978), p. 3.

[43]*Virginia State Board of Pharmacy v. Virginia Citizens Consumer Council,* 425 U.S. 478 (1976).

[44]*Virginia State Board of Pharmacy v. Virginia Citizens Consumer Council,* "Legal Developments in Marketing," *Journal of Marketing,* Vol. 41, No. 1 (January 1977), pp. 94-95.

[45]John F. Cady, "Advertising Restrictions and Retail Prices," *Journal of Advertising Research,* Vol. 16, No. 5 (October 1976), p. 29.

[46]Cady, Ibid.

was not protected by the First Amendment. In this landmark case, however, the Court indicated that commercial advertising should be protected by the First Amendment guarantee of free speech. According to the Court, if advertising "is indispensable to the proper allocation of resources in a free enterprise system, it is also indispensable to the formation of intelligent opinions as to how that system ought to be regulated or altered. Therefore, even if the First Amendment were thought to be primarily an instrument to enlighten public decision-making in a democracy, we could not say that the free flow of information does not serve that goal."

Although the Court declared restrictions on pharmaceutical advertising to be unconstitutional, it did not extend the ruling to include advertising of legal and medical services. In fact, the Court specifically stated that legal and medical advertising may require an examination of different considerations. In 1977, however, any doubt that the Court would retreat from its position in Virginia Board of Pharmacy was dispelled. In *Bates v. State Bar of Arizona,* the Supreme Court indicated that restrictions on the advertising of legal services is a violation of lawyers' constitutional right of free speech.[47] Two Arizona lawyers not only advertised that legal services at their clinic were available at reasonable rates, but also listed rates for numerous routine legal matters. In response to a disciplinary rule adopted by the State Bar of Arizona to restrict such advertising, the two lawyers were compelled to test the rule as an unconstitutional violation of the lawyers' right to free speech. Their efforts were successful.

Although the court reversed the Bar's rule on advertising of prices, it did not declare advertising restrictions to be *per se* violations of the First Amendment. In fact, the court indicated that its decision did not apply to advertising messages which allude to quality of service or personal solicitation methods such as in-hospital visits to obtain clients.

The implications of the court's decision in Bates may be widespread and significant. First, the immediate and direct impact of the decision is to afford consumers the opportunity to obtain information on cost and availability of legal services. Second, price advertising may subsequently lead to price competition and a reduction in the cost of legal service. Third, stimulation of demand and the attendant economies of scale which normally accompany advertising programs will probably be realized. Fourth, demand for lawyers will increase, and barriers to entry into the profession may be reduced. Fifth, the Bates decision suggests that other professional codes may also be unconstitutional and subject to modification. On the other hand, prior to finalization of the Bates decision, lawyers generally believed

[47]*Bates and O'Steen v. State Bar of Arizona,* "Legal Developments in Marketing," *Journal of Marketing,* Vol. 42, No. 1 (January 1978), pp. 108-109.

the impact would be negative. A study conducted to test lawyers' attitudes indicated that practicing lawyers are skeptical of advertising's ability to cause price declines, improvement in demand, and reductions in entry barriers.[48] In fact, the lawyers believed that the effect of a Bates decision would be to (1) "erode public confidence in the legal profession," (2) create deception, and (3) confuse clients.[49] As one Arizona Bar Association member remarked, "Advertising the law business leads to incompetence at best . . . and sometimes to . . . lying, cheating and swindling."[50]

As members of most professions anticipated, the wheel of change has continued to turn. In 1977 the FTC issued a complaint which alleged that the American Medical Association had been engaging in activities designed to restrain advertising by physicians.[51] Also in 1977, a New York orthodontist filed suit against the Board of Regents of the State University of New York and several dental associations for restricting her from advertising in the yellow pages of the telephone directory.[52] Finally, in 1978 the FTC promulgated a trade regulation rule on ophthalmic goods and services. Development of the rule represents the first attempt by the FTC to utilize its rule-making authority granted by Congress in the Magnuson-Moss Warranty—FTC Improvement Act of 1975. If successful in affecting the trade regulation rule, the FTC could keep states and consumer groups from restricting retail advertising of eyeglasses. In addition, an important procedural question will be dealt with: does an FTC trade regulation rule preempt state laws which restrict advertising of eyeglasses and eye examinations?[53]

Bait Advertising

Bait advertising is "an alluring but insincere offer to sell a product or service which the advertiser in truth does not intend or want to sell."[54] In a

---

[48]Terence Shimp and Robert Dyer, "How the Legal Profession Views Legal Service Advertising," *Journal of Marketing,* Vol. 42, No. 3 (July 1978), p. 77.

[49]Shimp and Dyer, Ibid.

[50]Dorothy Cohen, "Shingle is Lawyer's Only Selling Tool? Court To Rule," *Marketing News,* Vol. 10, No. 20 (April 22, 1977), p. 4.

[51]In re The American Medical Association, et. al., "Legal Developments in Marketing," *Journal of Marketing,* Vol. 42, No. 1 (January 1977), p. 109.

[52]*Joan C. Staker, D.D.S. v. Board of Regents of The State University of New York, Theodore M. Black, et. al.,* "Legal Developments in Marketing," *Journal of Marketing,* Vol. 42, No. 3 (July 1978), pp. 120-121.

[53]Dorothy Cohen, "FTC Preempts States in Rule on Eyeglasses," *Marketing News,* Vol. 12, No. 9 (November 3, 1978), p. 4; Also, Joseph P. Mathews, "FTC Seen Expanding Ads for Professions," *Marketing News,* Vol. 12, No. 8 (October 20, 1978), p. 3.

[54]*Guides Against Bait Advertising,* Trade Regulation Rule, Adopted November 24, 1959.

recent case, Sears allegedly advertised home appliances with no intention of attempting to sell the advertised items.[55] In fact, after luring customers into the store with an attractive "bait" advertisement, salesmen not only made no attempt to sell the advertised item but attempted to persuade customers to purchase higher-priced alternatives. Efforts to persuade customers to "switch" brands involved disparagement of the advertised brand. Sears subsequently agreed to a consent order which forbade them from using bait-and-switch advertising tactics, from disparaging advertised appliances, and from utilizing sales and display tactics which make the advertised appliance appear to be defective or inferior to competitive brands. Finally, Sears was ordered to maintain an inventory which is reasonably adequate to meet demand for sale items and to display a copy of the advertisement conspicuously in the home appliance department.

The FTC is unambiguously specific about its attitude toward bait-and-switch tactics. In its trade regulation rule the FTC maintains that an advertisement which does not represent a *bona fide* offer to sell the advertised product should not be released. Also, advertisements should not misrepresent the actual price, quality, or saleability of the product in such a manner that later, on disclosure of the true facts, the purchaser may be switched from the advertised product to another, more desirable product.

In addition to making deceptive offers to sell, it is also illegal to discourage customers from purchasing the advertised merchandise. Activities which indicate to the commission that bait-and-switch tactics were employed include the following:

- refusal to demonstrate or sell the product as advertised
- disparagement of any aspect of the advertised product or disparagement of services which accompany the product (i.e., credit, service, warranty, etc.)
- failure to maintain an inventory which is reasonably adequate to meet demand
- refusal to take orders for the advertised merchandise to be delivered within a reasonable period of time
- showing of a defective product
- use of compensation methods which discourage salespeople from selling the advertised product

Also, if advertised merchandise is not available at all outlets, these outlets must be listed in the ad.

The final step in bait advertising is the "after-sale switch." Although the retailer may apparently offer and sell the product in good faith, it may use

---

[55]In re Sears, Roebuck, and Co., "Legal Developments in Marketing," *Journal of Marketing,* Vol. 41, No. 2 (April 1977), p. 106.

after-sale tactics which cause the consumer to cancel the purchase. Among those "unselling" tactics which suggest that the retailer is effecting a "switch" are: (1) accepting a deposit for an advertised item, then switching the customer to a higher-priced item; (2) failure to make delivery within a reasonable period of time; (3) delivery of defective merchandise; or (4) after-sale disparagement of the product or related services.

Bait advertising is injurious to honest, competing retailers, and it can also be damaging to consumers and manufacturers. Consumers, on the one hand, are deceptively lured into a business only to be coerced into purchasing more expensive merchandise. For example, Wendelken-Simminger, a furniture retailer, advertised "a houseful of furniture for just $333.00." When a customer tried to take advantage of the offer, Wendelken-Simminger's salespeople showed no advertised furniture and, in fact, attempted to sell other, higher-priced furniture.[56] Manufacturers are also concerned about the injurious effects of such tactics. Retailers often use advertising money provided by manufacturers to run bait advertisements. When consumers inquire about the advertised item, the salesperson might disparage the nationally-branded item and, subsequently, attempt to coerce the customer into purchasing a higher-margin, private brand. Such selling tactics cause injury to the manufacturer's image and immediate sales volume. In response to these deceptive sales and advertising tactics, manufacturers such as Zenith have conducted advertising campaigns to warn consumers of bait tactics.[57]

Endorsements and Testimonials

An endorsement or testimonial is any advertising message which consumers perceive as reflecting the opinions, beliefs, or experiences of an individual, group, or institution.[58] Although any individual can endorse a product or service, some advertisers find it productive to utilize the services of motion picture celebrities, television stars, or sports personalities. Their ability to attract attention to the message and, in some cases, establish credibility are primary reasons for using Orson Welles to promote wine, Bruce Jenner to recommend Wheaties, and Karl Malden to endorse American Express travelers' checks.

---

[56]In re Wendelken-Simminger and Co., et. al., "Legal Developments in Marketing," *Journal of Marketing,* Vol. 39, No. 4 (October 1975), p. 87.

[57]"Growth of Bait and Switch Retailing Hurts Manufacturers," *Industry Week,* Vol. 182 (July—September 1974), pp. 25-26.

[58]Adapted from "Guides Concerning Use of Endorsements and Testimonials in Advertising," Tile 16:Part 255.

Since consumers rely on these endorsements when making purchase decisions, it is important that the endorser use the product and be qualified to make expert judgments. If a professional racing driver recommends a particular brand of tire or a professional tennis player recommends a racquet, the consumer believes that the professional's comments reflect the expert opinion of the endorser. When experts endorse products, the endorsement "must be supported by an actual exercise of his expertise in evaluating product features or characteristics."[59] An examination, therefore, must take place and be as extensive as would be necessary for another person with similar credentials as the endorser to support conclusions about the product or service. Also, if the endorser compares competing brands, then he or she must evaluate the selected brands. Finally, if an endorsement is made by an organization, the organization must employ selection procedures which will "ensure that the endorsement fairly reflects the collective judgment of the organization."[60]

If, on the other hand, one can reasonably ascertain that a message does not reflect the opinion of the announcer, the message is not an endorsement. A fictitious dramatization of housewives discussing the benefits of furniture waxes would, therefore, not be an endorsement. Also, if a person who is obviously a professional announcer speaks on behalf of an advertiser, the announcer's statement does not necessarily reflect the opinion of the announcer and, therefore, is not an endorsement.

In summary, there are several rules established by the FTC relative to endorsements.

(1) The endorser must use the product or service.

(2) The endorser must be qualified to make expert judgments.

(3) The endorsement must be supported by examination which is extensive enough to support conclusions.

(4) Comparisons can only be made if the endorser actually examines compared brands.

(5) Organizational endorsements must reflect the collective judgment of the membership.

(6) Announcements and fictitious dramatizations that obviously do not reflect actual opinions are not endorsements.

Special Bargains

Since many organizations often find it advisable to make special offers to the consuming public in order to stimulate demand, the FTC has found it

---

[59]"Guides," Ibid., Part 255:3.
[60]"Guides," Ibid., Part 255:4.

necessary to examine and interpret the legality of such representations. Normally, special promotions or bargains are presented as 2-for-1 sales, cents-off sales, multiple purchase discounts, or other special offerings. Regardless of the language utilized to describe the special deals, they generally suggest to the consumer that something is being offered "free" of charge or at a discount. The FTC's attitude toward such discounting programs is reflected in an interpretive industry guide concerning the use of the word "free" as well as the Fair Packaging and Labeling Act.

When used as a promotional tool, the word "free" means that the consumer pays nothing for the free item, and if receipt of the free item is tied to the purchase of another, physically identical item (i.e., buy 1—get 1 free), the tying item must be offered at a price which does not exceed "regular" price. The FTC considers "regular" price to be the lowest price at which the item was sold during the 30-day period immediately prior to commencement of the special bargain. If the bargain is an introductory offer and no "regular" price has been established, such a "buy 1—get 1 free" sale is probably not appropriate. It can, however, be implemented if the offerer discontinues the bargain after a limited time and continues to sell the tying product for the same price at which it was sold during the special, introductory sale.

Other specific regulations concerning utilization of the word "free" are as follows.

(1) All contingencies related to the receipt and retention of the "free" item must be conspicuously located and clearly delineated. Footnotes do not satisfy this requirement.

(2) The supplier is responsible for the reseller's actions relative to implementation of the special bargain.

(3) Areas in which the "free" promotion is not offered must be stated in the firm's advertising (for example, "the offer is only available through participating dealers").

(4) No "free" offer should be made for more than 6 months during any 12 month period. At least 50 days should elapse between offers, and no more than 3 offers should be made per year.[61]

Although the legality of "cents-off" sales and special introductory offers is similar to the regulation of "free" offers, there are additional guidelines concerning specific packaging and labeling requirements for companies utilizing "cents-off" and introductory deals. Specific delineation of such packaging and labeling requirements is beyond the scope of this text. It behooves companies, however, to review guidelines as specified in the Fair

---

[61]Federal Trade Commission, "Guide Concerning Use of the Word 'Free' and Similar Representations," (November 6, 1971).

Packaging and Labeling Act prior to implementation of such promotional programs.

Mock-Ups and Agency Liability

In a sixty-second commercial illustrating the effectiveness of Rapid Shave, Colgate-Palmolive placed the shaving cream on what the announcer said was a piece of sandpaper. Immediately after Rapid Shave was applied, the camera focused on the razor effortlessly and smoothly cutting through the alleged sandpaper. In actuality, however, the sandpaper was a plexiglass prop with sand applied to the surface. The prop or mock-up was used instead of the real thing because of the extensive presoaking necessary to soften sandpaper enough to be smoothly shaven. Also, television production quality was not good and the grain on sandpaper was not easily recognizable to viewing audiences. After several appeals, the Supreme Court ruled that Colgate-Palmolive must cease and desist from deceptively advertising products by:

> Presenting a test, experiment or demonstration that (1) is represented to the public as actual proof of a claim made for the product which is material to inducing its sale, and (2) is not in fact a genuine test, experiment, or demonstration being conducted as represented and does not in fact constitute actual proof of the claim, because of the undisclosed use and substitution of a mock-up or prop instead of the product, article or substance presented. . . .[62]

In essence, the Court indicated that it was sometimes legal to use props or mock-ups to compensate for deficiencies in television's reproduction methods, but it was not legal to use an "undisclosed" prop or test to show visual proof of a claim.

Because of significant advances achieved by television in reproduction methods and quality, the need for mock-ups and the significance of the court's decision concerning mock-ups have all but disappeared. The court, however, also dealt with a related issue which has had significant impact on advertisers and their agencies. Specifically, in Colgate-Palmolive the court indicated that advertising agencies are liable for advertising messages it develops. In rejecting the Bristol-Meyers' decision in which the agency was not considered responsible,[63] the Court indicated that the agency is generally responsible for the creation, writing, and production of advertising cam-

---

[62]*FTC v. Colgate-Palmolive Co.*, 380 U.S. 374 (1965); Also, UCC ¶71, 409 (April 1965).
[63]*FTC v. Bristol-Meyers, Young and Rubicam, Inc.*, 46 FTC 162 (1949).

paigns, while the advertisers simply monitor and approve the final product. It is, therefore, the agency and not the advertiser that often perpetrates deception and unfairness. The opinion in Colgate-Palmolive was confirmed in a subsequent decision in which the court stated that "the agency more so than its principal should have known whether the advertisements had the capacity to mislead or deceive the public. . . . Its responsibility for creating advertising cannot be shifted to the principal who is liable in any event."[64] The courts have also indicated, however, that although the agency is liable for messages it solely or jointly prepared, it is not responsible for messages of which it has no knowledge.[65]

In addition to placing responsibility with the advertiser and the agency, there is some indication that the FTC may make the retailer equally liable for disseminating false or misleading advertising material concerning food, drugs, devices, or cosmetics. In a recent case, Pay'n Save, a retail drug store chain, was accused of disseminating false and misleading advertising material by paying for the placement of ads in local media.[66] The advertisement suggested that one could lose weight by taking Porter and Dietsch's weight reduction tablets. The message also stated that the user would not have to change eating habits, when, in fact, reduction in caloric intake was a critical part of the total weight reduction plan. Although the FTC did not apply the decision to the advertising of other products, it did note that Congress should "impose higher obligations on disseminators-distributors of advertising for food, drugs, (medical) devices, and cosmetics (items which may carry a potential for injury to health and safety)."[67]

FTC Remedies for Deception

Prior to the 1970's, the FTC's primary weapon against deceptive practices was the cease and desist order and minimal fines for violation of orders. However, as the consumer movement gained momentum and researchers learned more about the lasting impact of ads on consumer beliefs and perceptions, FTC action to expand the breadth of alternative remedies was significantly accelerated.

[64]*FTC v. Merck & Co., Inc., et. al.,* 69 FTC 526 (1966).

[65]For a discussion, see: Linda D. Elrod, "The FTC: Deceptive Advertising and The Colgate-Palmolive Company," *Washburn Law Journal,* Vol. 12, No. 2 (Winter 1973), pp. 133-150.

[66]In re Porter and Dietsch, Inc., et. al., "Legal Developments in Marketing," *Journal of Marketing,* Vol. 42, No. 4 (October 1978), p. 90.

[67]Porter and Dietsch, Inc., Ibid.

Corrective Advertising

In 1969, a group of George Washington University law students (i.e., students opposing unfair practices) conceptualized and proposed a corrective advertising program which was designed to (1) inform consumers that purchase decisions were made with false information and (2) nullify competitive benefits which were realized by the offender. When Campbell Soup Company misrepresented the quantity of vegetables and meat in its soup by placing marbles in the advertised soup bowl, the Students Opposing Unfair Practices (SOUP) filed a motion to require that Campbell cease and desist the unfair advertising practice and inform consumers of these misleading tactics.[68]

Although the FTC rejected SOUP's proposed remedial action in the Campbell case, it did suggest that the approach had merit and, subsequently, included corrective advertising in several complaints including ITT Continental Baking Company (Profile bread), Coca Cola (Hi C), Standard Oil of California (F-310 gasoline additive), Ocean Spray Cranberries, Inc., American Home products Corporation (Anacin), Sun Oil Company, Bristol-Meyers Company (Excedrin), Warner-Lambert Company (Listerine), and Sugar Information, Inc.

In 1971 the Commission negotiated a consent agreement, including the corrective advertising requirement, with ITT Continental Baking Company. In recent advertising campaigns ITT Continental had strongly suggested that Profile bread had fewer calories than other brands and would, therefore, help one lose weight. In reviewing the claims, it was revealed that Profile had only 7 fewer calories per slice than competing brands, which was caused by producing thinner slices. As a result of the deception, ITT was required to spend 25 percent of its advertising budget for Profile bread to inform consumers that Profile does not have fewer calories than other breads and, therefore, does not help one lose weight.[69] Similar consent agreements were obtained from Ocean Spray Cranberries, Inc. (for misrepresenting the nutritional value of its fruit juice), and Sugar Information, Inc. (for misrepresenting the dietary value of sugar).[70]

Although the FTC successfully negotiated several consent agreements requiring corrective advertising, doubt surrounding the court's attitude toward this new FTC weapon was not disspelled until 1977 in *Warner-Lambert v. FTC*.[71] For over 50 years Warner-Lambert claimed in its adver-

---

[68]Campbell Soup Co. Trade Reg Reporter 19261, at 21421 (FTC 1970).

[69]*ITT Continental Baking Company*, 1973 CCH Transfer Binder, 19,681 (1971).

[70]*Ocean Spray Cranberries, Inc.*, 1973 CCH Transfer Binder, 19,981 (1972); *Sugar Institute*, 1973 CCH Transfer Binder, 20,142 (1972).

[71]*Warner-Lambert v. FTC*, 562 F. 2d (1977).

tisements that Listerine helped prevent colds and sore throats. Since Listerine does not have the necessary ingredients to affect viruses which cause colds, the Court ruled that the company would be required to state in future advertisements that "Listerine will not prevent colds or sore throats or lessen their intensity." Deviating from the "25 percent" rule applied in prior consent agreements, Warner-Lambert was required to include the phrase in all Listerine advertisements until $10 million had been spent.[72] This $10 million budget was equivalent to the average yearly advertising budget for Listerine during the 10 year period 1962 to 1972.

One of the significant results of Warner-Lambert was that the FTC was, for the first time, given the right to apply retrospective remedies (i.e., corrective advertising) as well as to attempt to restrict future deceptions. This decision to uphold corrective advertising is consistent with the Government's original dictum that the FTC should have wide latitude to respond to a changing business environment. A second significant result was that the contention that corrective advertising requirements violate the advertiser's First Amendment rights was dispelled. In fact, the Court stated that it is sometimes "appropriate to require that a commercial message appear in such a form, or include such additional information, warnings, and disclaimers as are necessary to prevent its being deceptive."[73]

An issue that was not resolved, however, involves the length of time an advertisement must appear before corrective advertising is needed to "dispell the residual affects of such deceptive advertising."[74] In Warner-Lambert one of the primary reasons corrective advertising was an appropriate remedy was the length of time with which Listerine had made its claims. In the Egg Nutrition case, however, a corrective statement was not needed because of the short length of time the deception prevailed.[75] How long must an ad appear before consumer attitudes are affected? At what point is competition injured? How long does it take to affect purchase intentions? Although there is research which suggests that corrective advertising may influence consumer attitudes and purchase intentions,[76] there is contradictory research which suggests that corrective advertising may have limited effect on purchase

---

[72]In prior consent decrees companies were required to spend 25 percent of their yearly advertising budget.

[73]*Virginia State Board of Pharmacy v. Virginia Citizens Consumer Council,* 425 U.S. 748 (1976); also, 1976-1, Trade Cases #60930.

[74]Dorothy Cohen, "Remedies for Consumer Protection: Prevention, Restitution, or Punishment," *Journal of Marketing,* Vol. 39, No. 4 (October 1975), p. 27.

[75]*Trade Cases,* 1977-2, 61751 (7th Cir. 1977).

[76]Harold H. Kassarjian, "Applications for Consumer Behavior to the Field of Advertising," *Journal of Advertising,* Vol. 3, No. 3 (1974), p. 14.

intentions.[77] To complicate the issue further, there is some indication that if a firm utilizes promotional resources to suggest in ads that the firm is interested in protecting consumer rights, the negative effects of subsequently run corrective advertisements may be intensified.[78] The complexity of the issue is evident and suggests that researchers and the FTC must conduct more conclusive studies to help policy makers determine future directions for corrective advertising.[79]

Finally, if corrective advertising is confirmed as an effective weapon against false and deceptive advertising, the costs of deception will be high. It was already noted that Listerine must place a corrective statement in $10 million of its advertising. If convicted, American Home Products may be required to spend $24 million to advertise that "Anacin is not a tension reliever."[80] Also, in *STP v. FTC*, STP agreed to pay $200,000 to advertise in several magazines that STP's tests cannot be relied on to substantiate claims that STP oil additive reduces oil consumption.[81] In addition, STP agreed to a $500,000 civil penalty for the false allegations. FTC notices (corrective ads) have appeared in such publications as the *New York Times, Newsweek, Wall Street Journal, People, and Forbes.*

Substantiation of Advertising Claims

Until June 1971, firms could, without substantial fear of FTC intervention, advertise various performance, safety, efficacy, quality, and comparative price claims which had no factual basis. Particularly in highly-competitive, mature industries, companies would advertise subtle and, in some cases, nonexistent variations in product to create the impression of brand uniqueness. Responding to consumer demands for accurate information with which to make rational decisions, the FTC adopted a resolution which requires firms to submit on demand documentation to substantiate advertising and product uniqueness claims. Information collected from advertisers by the FTC to support claims is subsequently presented to the public for inspection and comment.

Requests for company data relative to advertising claims and public

---

[77]William C. Rodgers, "The Corrective Advertising Remedy—Alternative Product and Consumer Interest Policy Dimensions," *Proceedings: Southern Marketing Association* (1978), pp. 109-111.

[78]Rodgers, Ibid.

[79]See: Dorothy Cohen, "Anacin Ruling Indicates Research Role at FTC," *Marketing News,* Vol. 12, No. 12 (December 15, 1978), p. 4. In 1978, the FTC mailed 14,000 questionnaires to consumers to determine the extent to which corrective advertising affected attitudes toward Listerine mouthwash.

[80]Cohen, Ibid.

[81]CCH ¶21390.

disclosure of unsupported claims is justified by the FTC for the following reasons. First, the disclosure of supporting data enables consumers to evaluate objectively the feasibility of claims and determine rationally the extent to which alternative brands can satisfy their needs. Second, advertisers are not voluntarily providing enough information with which to make informed purchase decisions. Third, companies can objectively evaluate and challenge the claims of competing firms, thus stimulating competition. Fourth, requiring complete documentation of claims will encourage companies to research, test, and justify product performance before such claims are advertised to the public. Finally, by publicly disclosing supporting information, the FTC obtains the aid of consumer groups, businesses, and consumers in detecting unsubstantiated claims. The FTC's limited resources are, therefore, supplemented.[82]

Since its adoption in 1971, the advertising substantiation program has become extensive with support data being requested from companies concerning such products as air conditioners, acne preparations, antiperspirants, automobiles, automobile tires, cold remedies, televisions, dental products, dishwashers, shampoos, electric shavers, hearing aids, pet food, power lawn mowers, soaps, and detergents. When the FTC issues a complaint against a company, it is the responsibility of the company to show that there is a "reasonable basis" for making the claim.[83] For example, Sears advertised its Lady Kenmore dishwasher as "the do-it-yourself dishwasher" which required "no scraping and no pre-rinsing." The FTC challenged Sears because there was no "reasonable basis" for making such claims.[84] In fact, the claims were inconsistent with instructions in the accompanying owner's manual which suggested that users pre-soak and scour baked-on foods.

Although the FTC has not delineated any specific guidelines or research procedures that should be observed when establishing a "reasonable basis" for advertising or uniqueness claims, it has indicated that scientific, objective, and acceptable research procedures be utilized. Also, the tests should be "extensive and well documented."[85]

In addition, advertising agencies are also liable for unsubstantiated

---

[82]Philip Borowsky, "The Federal Trade Commission and the Corrective Advertising Order," *University of San Francisco Law Review,* Vol. 6 (April 1972), pp. 375-376; also "FTC Resolution-Advertising Documentation," Commerce Clearing House, #7573.

[83]Robert E. Wilkes and James B. Wilcox, "Recent FTC Actions: Implications for the Advertising Strategist," *Journal of Marketing,* Vol. 38 (January 1974), pp. 55-56.

[84]In re Sears, Roebuck and Co., "Legal Aspects of Marketing," *Journal of Marketing,* Vol. 42, No. 3 (July 1978), p. 120.

[85]Wilkes and Wilcox, op. cit.; also, see for cases which reflect the Commission's thinking relative to the "reasonable basis" criterion.

advertising claims about products.[86] Prior to placing the advertisement, the agency must request (and maintain for three years after the ads are placed) documentation relative to the following in order for the agency to escape liability:

(1) The agency presented to the client, in writing, all reasonable interpretations of the advertisements and requested, in writing, any test, experiment, demonstration, study, or survey conducted by or in possession of the client which tends to support or disprove each of the interpretations.

(2) The agency neither knows nor had reason to know that the representations were false or that there was no reasonable basis for such representations.[87]

Affirmative Disclosure

In order to help consumers make more objective, informed purchase decisions, the FTC has instituted a program which requires that some advertisers disclose positive as well as negative product information. Although early FTC affirmative disclosure decisions were primarily directed at the food and drug industry to require disclosure of possible side effects or dangers and to provide package fill information, more recent action has been directed toward land deals,[88] computer schools,[89] hair replacement centers,[90] and tobacco companies.[91] The affirmative disclosure order which had the most widespread and significant impact was directed at the cigarette industry where advertisers must display in all ads the Surgeon General's warning of potential health hazards.

In *Keefe Hair and Scalp Specialists, Inc., v. FTC,* the 5th Circuit Court confirmed an FTC order requiring Keefe to state in future advertisements

[86]All commercial advertising is not affected by the Ad Substantiation Program. See: S. Prakash Sethi, "The Case (For and Against) the Imposition of Proof of Accuracy or Substantiation Requirements on Advocacy or Issue-Oriented Corporate Image Advertising," *Wayne Law Review,* Vol. 23, No. 4 (July 1977), pp. 1229-1259.

[87]In re Sears Roebuck and Co., "Legal Aspects of Marketing," *Journal of Marketing,* Vol. 42, No. 3 (July 1978), p. 120.

[88]In re Las Animas Ranch, Inc., et al.; Flagg Industries, Inc., et. al.; Roland International Corporation, et. al.; "Legal Developments in Marketing," *Journal of Marketing,* Vol. 41, No. 4 (October 1977), p. 111.

[89]Control Data Corp., et al.; Lear Siegle, Inc.; Electro Computer Programming Institute, et. al., "Legal Developments in Marketing," *Journal of Marketing,* Vol. 36, No. 4 (October 1972), p. 70.

[90]Medi Hair International, et al., "Legal Developments in Marketing," *Journal of Marketing,* Vol. 36, No. 4 (October 1972), p. 69.

[91]1973 CCH Transfer Binder 19,902 (1972).

that most baldness cases cannot be successfully treated.[92] Similarly, Hair Replacement Centers of Boston was required to advise customers of potential risks associated with hair implantation and display the following notice in future advertisements:

> Warning: This application involves surgery whereby sutures are placed in the scalp. Discomfort, pain and medical problems may occur. Continuing care is necessary. Consult your own physician.[93]

The land sales industry has also been the target for FTC activity to monitor and control deceptive sales and advertising practices. In *Las Animas Ranch, Inc., et. al.,* several Colorado-based land sales companies were directed to "clearly disclose in advertising and contracts the risk in purchasing land, the uncertainty of the land's value, and the advisability of contacting a qualified professional about the purchase."[94] In California, Flagg Industries was required to spend substantial amounts of money improving and maintaining its real estate subdivisions as well as affirmatively disclose "the buyer's right to cancel."[95] Finally, Roland International, a Florida land developer, was required to disclose the risks and uncertainties associated with purchasing underdeveloped land as an investment and was directed to advise customers to consult a qualified real estate professional before purchasing.[96]

Cooling-off Period

In addition to requiring affirmative disclosure, the FTC has frequently accompanied the disclosure order with a "cooling-off" directive. Hair Replacement Centers of Boston was directed to give customers 3 days in which to cancel contracts.[97] Las Animas Ranch was required to include a 10-day cooling-off period in contracts, and Roland International was required to provide a 10-day cooling-off period to cancel contracts and a 3-day cooling-off period after visiting the subdivision.[98]

Application of the cooling-off directive to restrict utilization of deceptive sales practices received formal commission approval in 1974 with adoption

---

[92]*Keefe Hair and Scalp Specialists, Inc. v. FTC,* 275 F. 2d 18 (8th Cir. 1970).

[93]In re Hair Replacement Centers of Boston, Inc. et al., "Legal Developments in Marketing," *Journal of Marketing,* Vol. 41, No. 1 (January 1977), pp. 96-97.

[94]In re Las Animas Ranch, Inc., et al.; Flagg Industries, Inc., et al.; Roland International Corporation, et al.; "Legal Developments in Marketing," *Journal of Marketing,* Vol. 41, No. 4 (October 1977), p. 111.

[95]Flagg Industries, Ibid.

[96]Roland International, Ibid.

[97]*Hair Replacement Centers of Boston, op. cit.*

[98]*Las Animas Ranch; Roland International, op. cit.*

of a trade regulation rule conceiving a *Cooling-Off Period for Door-to-Door Sales.*[99] The cooling-off rule requires sellers to print the following statement on contracts for the sale of consumer goods and services:

> You, the buyer, may cancel this transaction at any time prior to midnight of the third business day after the date of this transaction. See the attached notice of cancellation form for an explanation of this right.

A written notice which can be utilized by the consumer to cancel the contract must be attached to the contract, and consumer rights with respect to the terms of cancellation must be orally explained by the salesperson at the time of sale. The cooling-off rule only applies to sales made at locations other than the seller's place of business. It does not apply to telephone or mail transactions, the sale of insurance or securities, sales made at a retail facility where goods are displayed, or maintenance service at the buyer's home.

Consumer Redress

The Magnuson-Moss Warranty—FTC Improvement Act authorizes the FTC to obtain consumer redress when an individual or firm engages in an act or practice "which a reasonable man would have known under the circumstances was dishonest or fraudulent." The forms of relief that can be granted to consumers include recision or reformation of contracts, refund of money or return of property, payment of damages, and public notification.

Although not widely applied since passage of the law, the FTC has recently initiated action to exercise its authority. In one case, Glenn Turner was charged with defrauding consumers of millions of dollars through his pyramid marketing organization, Koscot Cosmetics.[100] When a finalized cease and desist was ordered against Koscot, the FTC reserved the right to obtain consumer redress and exercised that right in 1977. The FTC has also initiated a consumer redress action against Las Animas Ranch, which consented to stop misrepresenting investment potential of land it sold and the availability of utilities and services.[101] The recent FTC action seeks monetary damages and a reduction of the amount consumers owe the company for land they previously purchased.

---

[99]FTC Trade Regulation Rule, *Cooling-Off Period for Door-to-Door Sales,* Promulgated October 18, 1972, Effective June 7, 1974.

[100]In re Glenn W. Turner Enterprises and In re Koscot Interplanetary, Inc., "Legal Developments in Marketing," *Journal of Marketing,* Vol. 42, No. 4 (October 1978), p. 91.

[101]In re Las Animas Ranch, "Legal Developments in Marketing," *Journal of Marketing,* Vol. 42, No. 4 (October 1978), p. 91.

Fines and Injunctive Relief

The FTC Act as amended in 1973 by the TransAlaska Pipeline Authorization Act increased the maximum fine for violation of a cease and desist order from $5,000 to $10,000 and authorized the FTC to obtain temporary injunctions against Section 5 violations. Considered to be a relatively ineffective method of deterring deceptive behavior, the $10,000 fine can only be issued after a cease and desist order has been violated. In most cases, damage caused by deceptive or false activity has already been realized at the time a cease and desist order is issued. If the order is subsequently violated, however, a fine of $10,000 per day can be levied, since each day the order is violated represents a separate violation.

Preliminary injunctive authority was granted to the FTC in order to safeguard the public's interest by immediately stopping false, deceptive, and unfair behavior. In order to obtain an injunction against false advertising, it is necessary that the court first consider the likelihood that the FTC will be successful in proving that the activity is actually false or misleading.[102] After an assessment is made of the potential legality of the advertising message, the court must balance the positive and negative implications of injunctive relief. In one case, the FTC charged that Simeon Management Corporation was engaging in false advertising by failing to disclose that a weight loss program actually involved injections of a drug and that the drug had never been proven to be more effective or safe than a dietary program.[103] Since these facts were not disclosed to the public and would have possibly been influential in consumers' purchase decisions, the FTC considered the advertising message misleading. In response to the FTC allegations, the court indicated that it is unnecessary to include all facts relevant to a purchasing decision in an advertisement. Also, since the drug was not mentioned in Simeon's ads, the consumer was not being deceived into believing that the weight loss program was more effective than it really was. Since the ads were probably not deceptive and the weight loss program had proven to be effective in helping many patients lose weight, the court found that the equities in the case outweighed the issuance of an injunction.

Self-Regulation of Advertising

Although government regulation of advertising has expanded substantially during the 1970's, advertisers' efforts to police constituent activities

---

[102]FTC v. Simeon Management Corporation, et al., "Legal Developments in Marketing," *Journal of Marketing,* Vol. 40, No. 4 (October 1976), p. 117.

[103]FTC v. Simeon Management Corporation, et al., Ibid.

have experienced similar growth and success. In fact, in 1971 the American Advertising Federation, the American Association of Advertising Agencies, the Association of National Advertisers, and the Council of Better Business Bureaus established the National Advertising Review Board (NARB) to implement a program of self-regulation. As an intermediary organization between consumers and the Federal Government, the NARB is charged with the responsibility of maintaining high standards of honesty and accuracy in national advertising.

Complaints regarding the truth and accuracy of ads are initially submitted by consumers, consumer groups, industrial organizations, or advertising firms to the NARB's investigative staff, the National Advertising Division (NAD). After a complaint is filed, the NAD evaluates the legitimacy of the complaint and, if it is justified, subsequently attempts to resolve the problem constructively. If the advertiser and/or advertising agency is unwilling to change or withdraw the advertisement, the complaint is appealed to the NARB, the primary regulatory group consisting of 30 members representing national advertisers, 10 members representing advertising agencies, and 10 members representing public or non-industry fields. Upon receipt of the appeal, the Chairman of the NARB appoints a 5-person panel from the membership to resolve the issue. After reviewing both the NAD's findings and the advertiser's counterarguments, the NARB panel arrives at a decision which is communicated to the top executive level of the offending firm. If, after exhausting all appropriate remedies, the advertiser still is unwilling to accept the NARB's decision, the Federal Government is informed of the violation.

The NARB has been successful in monitoring false and misleading advertising and in setting a state-by-state precedent toward self-regulation. In its first year of operation, the NARB got 84 advertisers to withdraw or modify ads. In 1976, utilization of an NARB-type organization to persuade advertisers to conform to standards of honesty and accuracy was given support by a Colorado district court in a case involving the advertising of Pat Walker's weight reduction center. Specifically, Ve-Ri-Tas, Inc., leased 15 weight reduction machines to Pat Walker's of Denver. With rental of the equipment, Pat Walker's also received advertising material from the lessor which, according to the Denver Advertising Review Board (ARB), was misleading.[104] In order to coerce the companies into conforming to acceptable advertising standards, the BBB and ARB threatened to issue a news

---

[104]Ve-Ri-Tas, Inc. and Pat Walker's of Colorado, Inc., v. Advertising Review Board of Metropolitan Denver, Inc., Rocky Mountain Better Business Bureau, Inc., Advertising Club of Denver, et al., "Legal Developments in Marketing," *Journal of Marketing,* Vol. 41, No. 2 (April 1977), pp. 104-105.

release detailing Pat Walker's deceptive activities. Pat Walker's and Ve-Ri-Tas subsequently attempted to stop the agency's regulatory action by arguing, in court, that it has First Amendment protection of free speech and that the ARB and BBB were engaging in antitrust activity. Concerning the "First Amendment" argument, the court indicated that Pat Walker's did have protection of free speech,[105] but the ARB and BBB were also protected by the First Amendment and, therefore, had the right to "call public attention to the offending conduct."[106] To restrict the ARB and BBB from advertising their attitudes toward a commercial message would be to compromise their right to First Amendment protection. Also, relative to the antitrust accusation, the court indicated that no violation had been committed since neither the ARB nor the BBB attempted to boycott or persuade others to boycott Pat Walker's business. The decision of the district court was subsequently affirmed by the Appeals Court,[107] and the Supreme Court refused to review the case.[108]

In addition to the efforts of the NARB, NAD, and similar local advertising review boards, self-regulation has also been supported by the Better Business Bureaus, advertising agencies, and advertising media. The BBB has been one of the most effective agencies for monitoring and publicizing unfair and deceptive practices. Supported by local businessmen, the BBB investigates complaints, attempts to persuade offenders to stop unfair practices, and, if necessary, employs legal remedies. In addition, the BBB provides businesses with advice concerning the legal aspects of advertising.

Since advertising agencies can also be liable for the false and misleading advertisements of their clients, they have, like many advertisers, instituted internal programs of self-regulation by monitoring copy, demanding substantiation of claims from clients, and extensively utilizing legal counsel. In addition, the American Association of Advertising Agencies co-sponsored organization of the NARB and maintains a committee for monitoring and policing questionable advertising practices. Self-regulation by advertising media has taken the form of (1) bans on unacceptable ads and (2) industry codes or guides. For example, the television code of the National Association of Broadcasters states that "television broadcasters should, in recognition of their responsibility to the public, refuse the facilities of their stations to an advertiser where they have good reason to doubt the integrity of the adver-

[105]See: *Virginia State Board of Pharmacy v. Virginia Citizens Consumer Council*, CCH 60930 (Sup. Ct. 1976).

[106]*Ve-Ri-Tas, Inc.*, p. 105.

[107]Ve-Ri-Tas, Inc., et al., "Legal Developments in Marketing," *Journal of Marketing*, Vol. 42, No. 3 (July 1978), p. 121.

[108]Ve-Ri-Tas, Inc., et al., "Legal Developments in Marketing," *Journal of Marketing*, Vol. 42, No. 4 (October 1978), p. 91.

tiser, the truth of the advertising representations, or the compliance of the advertiser with the spirit and purpose of all applicable legal requirements."[109] The code goes on to specify products which cannot be advertised, guidelines which should be followed in presenting ads, and guidelines for offering contests, premiums, and offers.

Summary

In 1938, Congress enacted the Wheeler-Lea Act to sanction the Federal Trade Commission as a consumer protection agency. Although the FTC continued to protect business from anticompetitive behavior, it now had an additional responsibility to protect consumers from deceptive practices of business. It accomplished this goal by monitoring promotional activities of businesses and by investigating complaints submitted by consumers, government agencies, and other businesses.

One of the FTC's primary functions is to regulate advertising messages of sellers in order to determine if they have the capacity to deceive ultimate consumers. It is unnecessary to prove that the advertisement does, in actuality, deceive. All the FTC must do is show that it has the capacity to deceive. Also, the possible deception may be implied rather than explicitly stated.

During the 1970's, advertisers have witnessed numerous significant legal developments in advertising. Generally, these developments have related to (1) FTC remedies for deceptive practices, (2) comparison advertising, (3) advertising of professional services, and (4) advertising to children. Advertising to children received FTC attention in the form of a proposed trade regulation rule. The rule, proposed in 1978, would restrict advertising directed at young children and would require affirmative disclosure of the nutritional value of some sweetened products. In addition to the rule, the FTC has actively attacked advertisements that may induce children to engage in dangerous activity and is moving to restrict the use of hero figures and premiums to sell to children.

Comparison advertising involves the comparison of 2 or more competing brands. Although there are no specific laws designed to restrict comparison advertising, it can be attacked as an unfair method of competition under the FTC Act. Most efforts during the 1970's have been directed at understanding its implications and developing guidelines for self-regulation. As

[109]"The Television Code," National Association of Broadcasters, 19th edition (June, 1976) in *Legal and Business Problems of the Advertising Industry,* 1978, Practicing Law Institute (New York, 1978), p. 76.

long as the advertiser is honest in its comparison and can substantiate claims with scientific tests, the FTC will probably not impose regulations.

Advertising of professional services has traditionally been restricted by the various professional associations' codes of ethics. In 1976, however, the Supreme Court declared that rules designed to restrict advertising of pharmaceutical drug prices is a violation of the advertiser's right of free speech. In 1977, the court made a similar ruling directed at the legal profession. Although these rulings do not extend to other professions, there have been actions initiated against the American Medical Association, dental associations, and the opthalmic industry.

Although numerous advances in self-regulation of the advertising industry have been made in the 1970's, methods for nullifying negative results of a deceptive message have not been effectively implemented within the industry. The FTC has therefore advanced several retrospective remedies. First, the corrective advertising remedy requires that the advertiser inform consumers of a deception. Second, the FTC may require that an advertiser substantiate claims with sufficient documentation and inform consumers of any unsubstantiated claims. Third, the FTC may require that advertisers affirmatively disclose positive as well as negative information about a product.

Discussion Questions

1. The FTC has defined a deceptive advertisement as one which has the capacity to deceive. Although puffery is not currently illegal, can it be argued that ads which employ puffing tactics have the capacity to deceive?

2. Should the government strengthen and expand its controls over advertising?

3. Do you believe that the cooling-off rule will positively and/or negatively influence a salesman's closing rate?

4. Develop a methodology for identifying deception in an advertisement.

5. Do you think that companies should be allowed to engage in comparison advertising?

6. What variables have contributed most significantly to the expansion of advertising regulation?

6 PRODUCT-RELATED DECISIONS

One author describes a product as a "complex of tangible and intangible attributes . . . which the buyer may accept as offering satisfaction of wants or needs."[1] Attributes which make up and describe products may include, among other things, brand name, label, physical characteristics, warranty, and package. Successful development of these attributes into a product is primarily contingent upon the producer's ability to match perceived product benefits with the needs and desires of consumers.

Since product development is the primary input variable for long-run growth and profits, much pressure is placed on marketers to insure that attributes do, in fact, satisfy consumer wants. They may use certain color combinations to suggest product benefits or imply the existence of value benefits with large packages which are not completely filled, unidentified ingredients which are not consistent with the quality expectations of consumers, costly safety features which may not be perceived as important to consumers, or impressive warranties which are significantly limited by "fine print" disclaimers.

In order to protect consumers from these deceptive practices as well as inform them of actual product characteristics and benefits, the Government and courts have developed a set of product-related rules which relate to product safety, packaging, labeling, warranties, and trademarks.

Product Safety

Prior to 1916, the issue of product safety was largely ignored, and redress for consumers who suffered injuries because of product defects or

---

[1] William J. Stanton, *Fundamentals of Marketing,* McGraw-Hill Book Company (New York, 1975), p. 171.

113

malfunctions was, for all practical purposes, nonexistent. The primary problem with obtaining redress was that the law made the manufacturer liable only to customers with whom the manufacturer transacted directly. The philosophy, known as *privity of contract,* relieved the manufacturer of any liability for sales made through middlemen. In 1916, however, the court established that the manufacturer was responsible to consumers for the negligent manufacturing of products, irrespective of contract.[2]

Although *McPherson v. Buick Motor Company* resolved the issue of privity of contract, it also established that consumers could successfully sue only if the manufacturer was negligent in its production of a consumer good. Since negligence was extremely difficult to prove, consumers usually could not win and manufacturers were not directed by law to insure that consumer products were safe for use. The 1916 ruling of the court, therefore, mandated the prevailing concept of *caveat emptor* and helped contribute to the 20 million accidents, 110,000 disabilities, and 30,000 deaths each year related to the use of consumer products.[3]

Strict Liability

One response to the problem of product safety came from the California Supreme Court in 1963. When Greenman used a combination power tool as a lathe to make a chalice, the tool malfunctioned and the block flew out and struck Greenman on the forehead. Upon evaluation of the case, the Supreme Court indicated that negligence is irrelevant in a case of strict product liability. As indicated by Justice Traynor, "a manufacturer is strictly liable in tort when an article he places on the market, knowing that it is to be used without inspection for defects, proves to have a defect that causes injury to a human being . . . . The purpose of such liability is to insure that the costs of injury resulting from defective products are borne by the manufacturers that put such products on the market rather than by the injured persons who are powerless to protect themselves."[4]

The philosophy of strict liability also states that it does not matter if the seller "exercised all possible care in the preparation and sale of his product."[5] The manufacturer is still liable for injuries to consumers who use the product. In addition, the reasonableness of the consumer's or seller's actions or knowledge is not an issue in strict liability cases.

To prove liability one must show (1) that the product had a manufactur-

---

[2]*McPherson v. Buick Motor Company,* CCH Products Liability Reports, ¶4504 (1916).

[3]Donald P. Rothschild and David W. Carroll, *Consumer Protection: Text and Materials,* Second Edition, Anderson Publishing Company (Cincinnati, 1977), p. 365.

[4]*Greenman v. Yuba Power Products, Inc.,* CCH Products Liability Reporter, ¶4510 (1963).

[5]Section 402A of the *Restatement of Torts.*

ing or design defect, and (2) the defect was the cause of the injury. Although it may seem difficult to prove that a defect was the specific cause of injury, a recent court ruling suggested that a defect is indicated by the malfunction itself. If a malfunction occurs, there is obviously a defect. Once the fact is established that the defect exists, the jury can assume the manufacturer was negligent and, therefore, strictly liable in tort. Specifically, Kridler purchased a Ford which he had to return to the dealer 24 times because of steering difficulties. Because of the apparent defect in the car's tie rod, Kridler eventually lost control and had a wreck. Although the lower court suggested that the evidence was insufficient to prove that a defect in the car caused the accident, the Appellate Court reversed the decision stating that "the existence of a malfunction alone . . . establishes a defective condition, and the plaintiff must prove only that the malfunction of the automobile was the proximate cause of the accident."[6]

Also in cases involving design defects, once the plaintiff identifies a defect and establishes that the defect was the proximate cause of injury, it is the responsibility of the manufacturer (i.e., defendant) to prove "in light of the relevant factors, that on balance the benefits of the challenged design outweigh the risk of danger inherent in such design."[7] Placing burden of proof on manufacturers adds another dimension to product development decisions. Specifically, manufacturers should be capable of proving the design is the best that it can be and that the benefits of the design outweigh potential dangers.[8] Simple introduction of evidence to suggest that the design might be the best it could be is not enough; rather, absolute proof and documentation of benefits are required.

Defense: Unforeseeable Abnormal and Unintended Use

If a product is used in a manner that is unintended or unforeseeably abnormal, the manufacturer is generally not responsible for accidents which occur during its misuse. For example, if a housewife splashes cleaning fluid into her eyes or a consumer uses a lawnmower to trim hedges, the manufacturers would not be liable.[9] If the misuse could have reasonably been foreseen by the manufacturer and adequate warning statements were not provided, however, the manufacturer is strictly liable. Also, if the product has a defect, foreseeability is not an issue. The manufacturer is strictly

[6]*Kridler v. Ford Motor Company,* CCH Product Liability Reporter, ¶6319 (1970).

[7]*Barker v. Lull Engineering Co., Inc., et al.,* CCH Products Liability Reporter, ¶8101.

[8]Paul Busch, "Product Liability Found in Machine Design," *Marketing News,* Vol. 12, No. 10, (November 17, 1978), p. 3.

[9]William L. Trombetta and Timothy L. Wilson, "Foreseeability of Misuse and Abnormal Use of Products by the Consumer," *Journal of Marketing,* Vol. 39 (July 1975), pp. 49-50.

liable, even for all the "unforeseen consequences thereof no matter how remote."[10]

Utilization of appropriate warning statements is significant if a manufacturer expects to escape liability for misues of its product. The statement should suggest what should be done to minimize risk and the potential consequences of its misuse. For example, a manufacturer of charcoal warned customers not to use its briquets in unventilated areas. When a lady used the charcoal in an unventilated room, she died of carbon monoxide poisoning.[11] Although the warning described actions that should be avoided, it did not indicate the consequences of such use (i.e., carbon monoxide poisoning). The manufacturer was, therefore, liable.

It is also important to use current "state of the art" technology to minimize the risk of injury and, at the same time, alleviate the probability of being considered liable for uses of the product in an unintended manner. When a driver was injured in a head-on collision while driving a Corvair, the manufacturer argued that it did not have a duty to manufacture a car which is injury-proof since the intended use of a car is not "colliding with other cars."[12] Evidence in the case suggested, though, that severe injury was more probable with the Corvair's solid shaft steering column than with other steering assemblies which are designed to guard against direct, rearward displacement in the event of a head-on collision. The court agreed that the Corvair's design created a hazard in excess of normal hazards associated with alternative designs and emphasized that it is the duty of the manufacturer to "design the product so that it will fairly meet any emergency or use which can reasonably be anticipated."

Although utilization of "state of the art" technology to avoid harm to consumers is advisable, it is not always a defense. In *Cunningham v. MacNeal Memorial Hospital,* a patient was given blood which, unknown to the hospital or patient, was infected with hepatitis virus.[13] Although there was no known method of detecting the virus in blood, the court indicated that the hospital was still responsible for the defective and impure product. The court was also careful to differentiate this situation from situations where a procedure is inherently dangerous when used in the manner that it was intended. For example, rabies vaccine produces serious reactions but is justified when correctly applied to save one's life. The difference in the two

[10]*Berkebile v. Brandley Helicopter,* CCH Products Liability Reporter, ¶7456 (1975).

[11]Arnold Bennigson, "Product Liability-Producers and Manufacturers Beware," *Research Management,* Vol. 18 (March 1975), p. 18.

[12]*Larsen v. General Motors Corporation,* CCH Products Liability Reporter, ¶5939 (1968).

[13]*Cunningham v. MacNeal Memorial Hospital,* CCH Products Liability Reporter, ¶6426 (1970).

situations is that the rabies vaccine is used in the manner that was intended while the blood was defective and "unreasonably dangerous to the user."

Defense: Contributory Negligence

Another potential defense occurs when the consumer is aware of a potentially-dangerous aspect of a product but still voluntarily risks using the product (contributory negligence). Although contributory negligence is not a defense when the consumer simply fails "to discover the defect in the product, or to guard against the possibility of its existence," it may be a defense when the consumer is "voluntarily and unreasonably proceeding to encounter a known danger."[14] For example, a consumer purchased a motor bike and immediately noticed a shimmy in the front wheel. Knowing that the wheel was defective, the user voluntarily proceeded to encounter the danger by continuing to ride the bike. When the defective part subsequently malfunctioned, the consumer could not successfully sue the manufacturer because he was aware of the defect and voluntarily assumed risk associated with its use.[15]

The court's attitude toward contributory negligence in strict liability cases may be changing. In one case, a printing press operator suffered hand injuries when he reached into a press to remove a foreign object without turning off the machine.[16] The Appeals Court suggested that, by reaching into an operating machine, the operator assumed a risk which was well-known by both the trade and the operator. The New York Supreme Court disagreed. The court indicated that the user is not necessarily responsible for injuries which occur when operating a potentially dangerous item. In a mechanized society it is mandatory that manufacturers take due care to provide necessary safety devices to guard against foreseeable injuries resulting from both intended and unintended use. Since the press manufacturer did not provide available hand safety devices designed to keep operators from chasing foreign items while the machine is in use, it was liable even though the operator's actions contributed to the accident.

Although the New York Supreme Court charged manufacturers with responsibility to take all available and necessary precautions to alleviate the probability of injury, the Illinois Supreme Court assumed a different position. In *Rios v. Niagara Machine and Tool Works,* the plaintiff was injured by a punch press manufactured by Niagara.[17] Although the machine was sold

---

[14]Emanuel Emrock, "Pleading and Proof in a Strict Product Liability Case," *Insurance Law Journal,* (October 1966), p. 593.

[15]*Bennigson,* p. 18.

[16]*Micallef v. Miehle Company, et. al.,* CCH Products Liability Reporter, ¶7701 (1976).

[17]*Rios v. Niagara Machine and Tool Works,* 59 Ill. 2d 79, 319 N.E. 2d 232 (1974).

without a safety device, the purchaser installed an appropriate device prior to the accident. In a ruling which places more responsibility on negligent users, the court indicated that the manufacturer was not liable because the purchaser installed a safety device which corrected any unsafe conditions which may have existed.[18] Also, the court could not establish that the failure of the purchaser-installed safety device was caused by the manufacturer's failure to provide a factory-installed device.[19] The decision is an obvious departure from the court's previous philosophy that manufacturers should take all possible precautions to insure against injury and that manufacturers cannot delegate responsibility for product safety to purchasers. In fact, in past cases manufacturers have consistently been held liable when industrial users remove safety devices which were originally installed by the manufacturer. Until Rios, if a manufacturer could reasonably foresee an intervening act such as removing a safety device, the manufacturer was consistently considered to be liable for injuries sustained after the third-party intervention.

A final development which will have significant impact on a plaintiff's ability to claim damages when contributory negligence or assumption of risk is present is the idea of "comparative fault." As indicated in the Uniform Comparative Fault Act, if an injury is partially or completely caused by the injured person's negligence or recklessness (i.e., contributory fault), the dollar amount of damages which can be recovered by the injured person is proportionately reduced by the extent of contributory fault attributed to the injured person. In one case, a driver of a pickup was injured when a carburetor malfunction caused the pickup to turn over.[20] During the trial General Motors pointed out that the malfunction was created by changes which were made in the carburetor by the plaintiff. The Texas Supreme Court ruled in favor of the injured driver's claim but reduced its size by the percentage of injury caused by his own misuse.[21] Although the case has not received unanimous support in other states, many observers believe the approach is a good start to needed reform in the strict liability law.

---

[18]Rima L. Skorubskas, "Strict Liability: An Unwarranted Limitation Upon the Manufacturer's Duty to Produce a Reasonably Safe Product," *DePaul Law Review*, Vol. 25 (Winter 1976), p. 535.

[19]Skorubskas, Ibid.

[20]*General Motors Corp. v. Hopkins*, 548 S.W. 2d 344 (Tex. 1977).

[21]See: *Mercer Law Review*, Vol. 24 (Winter 1978), John Wade, Products Liability and Plaintiff's Fault: The Uniform Comparative Fault Act," pp. 373-402; Aaron Twerski, "The Many Faces of Misuse: An Inquiry Into the Emerging Doctrine of Comparative Causation," pp. 403-436; John F. Vargo, "The Defenses to Strict Liability in Tort: A New Vocabulary With an Old Meaning," pp. 447-464.

Defense: No Defect

A final defense is that a design or a manufacturing defect did not exist when the product left the manufacturer's control. A purchaser of rifle cartridges was injured when his rifle was exploded by allegedly-defective cartridges.[22] Upon examination of the cartridges, however, there was evidence that they had possibly been reloaded by the user and, therefore, not necessarily defective when in the control of the manufacturer. Since there was "lack of evidence that the cartridge was defective when it left the manufacturer's possession, and there was evidence pointing to the fact that the purchaser may have been using a reloaded cartridge," the manufacturer was not liable.

Costs of Strict Liability

The costs associated with being strictly liable for a product malfunction can be high. In 1977, for example, U.S. manufacturers of football helmets were being sued for $110 million which represented 110 times their combined profits.[23] In another case, a tractor trailer pulling a pressurized propane tank swerved to avoid a head-on collision. During the maneuver, the tank broke from the tractor, exploded, killed 16 people, and injured an additional 44. After the court found that the fifth wheel, which held the tank to the tractor, was defective and that the center of gravity on the tank was too high, it declared that both manufacturers each pay $25 million to the various plaintiffs.[24]

Associated with the high costs of conviction are high insurance costs. Product liability insurance premium payments increased from $1.13 billion in 1975 to $2.75 billion in 1976.[25] A sporting goods manufacturer, for example, experienced a yearly premium increase from $1,000 to $225,000 in 5 years.[26] The propane tank manufacturer that was partially responsible for a $50 million settlement watched its premium increase from $30,000 for $20 million of insurance to approximately $350,000 for $3.5 million of insurance.[27] Even with these significant increases in premium charges, insurance companies lost approximately $9 billion on product liability claims from January 1974 to December 1976.[28]

---

[22]*Sundet v. Olin Mathieson Chemical Corporation,* CCH Products Liability Reporter, ¶5495 (1966).

[23]Paul Busch, "Football Helmet Makers Are Finding Product Liability a Kick in The Head," *Marketing News,* Vol. 11, No. 11 (December 3, 1977), p. 3.

[24]"The Devils in The Product Liability Laws," *Business Week,* (February 12, 1979), pp. 72-73.

[25]"Devils," Ibid., p. 72.

[26]Busch, *op. cit.*

[27]*Business Week, op. cit.*

[28]Product Liability—The Search for Solutions," *Nation's Business* (June 1977), p. 25.

The effect of recent developments in product liability and their associated costs has been significant. Companies have discontinued operations, realized declining profits, expanded quality control efforts, restricted the development of new products that are even slightly dangerous, and passed associated costs on to consumers. Marketers must now consider as one of their primary decision variables the probability of defect or malfunction and the costs associated with a potential malfunction. Persons responsible for quality control must insure that products do not leave the plant with potentially hazardous defects. Design engineers must anticipate all anticipated and unexpected uses for products and design products to minimize risk associated with the identified use. Finally, marketers must conspicuously relate all potentially hazardous aspects of the product to consumers.

State Legislatures Reduce Liability

In order to protect companies from the unreasonable hardships and possible destruction that can accompany a product liability suit, many state legislatures have enacted laws which limit manufacturers' liability. In at least 13 states reform bills have passed, and in most other states bills are either pending or being debated.

State laws, in essence, provide for a statute of limitations in liability cases, a defense that the product met federal standards when it left control of the manufacturer, and a defense that the product was altered by someone other than the manufacturer.[29] For example, the Utah Product Liability Act provides for a statute of limitations on product liability claims of 6 years from the date of initial purchase or 10 years from the date of manufacture. Second, complaints cannot specify the dollar amount of damages sought by the claimant. Third, contributory negligence, misuse, or product alteration are defenses in product liability cases. Fourth, no defect exists unless a defect which made the product unreasonably dangerous existed at the time that the product was initially sold. Finally, if the manufacture and sale of a product conform to government standards which exist when it is manufactured, the product can be considered defect-free.[30]

Consumer Product Safety Act

Created by Congress in 1967 to study problems associated with product safety and develop strategies to alleviate identified problems, the National Commission on Product Safety proposed that an agency be mandated to monitor and regulate matters exclusively related to product safety. The

[29]"Product Liability Score Card," *Business Week,* Vol. 12 (June 26, 1978), pp. 36-37.

[30]Charles W. McGrady and Ray McKenzie, "State Legislative Restrictions on Product Liability Actions," *Mercer Law Review,* Vol. 29 (Winter 1978), pp. 623-625.

agency which became known as the Consumer Product Safety Commission (CPSC) was formed in 1972 with passage of the Consumer Product Safety Act (CPSA).

The CPSC is administered by five commissioners who are appointed by the President for seven-year terms. Reporting to the commissioners are the executive director and directors of the 16 other areas of the commission. Several of the more significant divisions of the CPSC are the Bureau of Epidemiology, the Office of Field Coordination, and the Office of Standards Coordination and Appraisal. The Bureau of Epidemiology collects data on consumer product-related injuries through its National Electronic Injury Surveillance System (NEISS) and helps establish regulatory priorities. By analyzing data received from hospitals on consumer product-related injuries, the bureau develops a Product Hazard Index for products which should receive immediate commission attention. (In 1974, the ten most hazardous products included (1) bicycles, (2) stairs, (3) doors, (4) cleaning agents, (5) tables, (6) beds, (7) football equipment, (8) playground equipment, (9) liquid fuels, and (10) architectural glass.[31]) The Office of Field Coordination directs the enforcement activities of its 14 field offices and is responsible for coordinating its efforts with the efforts of state, local, and, federal agencies. The Office of Standards Coordination and Appraisal develops and manages the labeling requirements and product safety standards established by the CPSC.[32] Other divisions of the commission develop quality control standards for products, performance specifications, programs to alleviate injuries caused by chemical products, economic data related to product injuries and their attendant costs, programs on consumer education, and data which reflect the impact of safety standards on injuries.[33]

Consumer Interaction

To be consistent with its mission of consumer protection and service, the CPSC provides the public with all memoranda, documents, and reports relative to its operation. Also, it disseminates information through media concerning various consumer product hazards and ways to reduce the possibility of injury. Much of this consumer information is in the form of specific warnings about the hazards of using certain "dangerous" products. In addition to using the media to accomplish its information dissemination

[31]See: Paul Busch, "A Review and Critical Evaluation of the Consumer Product Safety Commission: Marketing Management Implications," *Journal of Marketing*, Vol. 40, No. 4 (October 1976), pp. 42-43.

[32]Donald P. Rothschild and David W. Carroll, *Consumer Protection: Text and Materials*, 2nd Ed., Anderson Publishing Co. (Cincinnati, 1977), p. 366.

[33]Rothschild and Carroll, Ibid., p. 367.

program, the CPSC has also instituted a telephone "Hot Line" program to answer consumer questions on product safety.

Safety Rules

One of the most significant aspects of the act gives the commission authority to adopt safety standards for consumer products.[34] With the express purpose of reducing risk of injury, product safety standards may be developed by (1) the commission or (2) an outside individual or agency. When a product standard is identified as reasonably necessary, the CPSC publishes its intent to develop such a standard in the *Federal Register*. The notice identifies the commission's intent to establish a standard and represents an invitation for anyone to develop a relevant rule or submit an existing rule. Persons who submit an offer to develop a standard are judged and selected on their technical competence, ability to develop a standard within the 150-day time limit established by Congress, and intention to comply with all commission regulations.[35] Finally, in order to facilitate the development of a more satisfactory standard, the CPSC may assume some of the offeror's cost of developing the standard.

Product Bans

If a product presents an unreasonable risk of injury and if no available safety standard will adequately protect consumers from dangers associated with the product, the CPSC may develop a rule which declares the product to be a banned hazardous product. The act also forbids manufacturers from stockpiling an affected product to avoid a product ban or safety rule.

In addition to products which present an "unreasonable risk of injury," the CPSA identified two additional categories of hazardous products: products creating a "substantial hazard" and products creating an "imminent hazard." Substantial hazards are created when a company fails to comply with a consumer product safety rule or the product has a serious defect. To facilitate identification of products that create a substantial hazard, the act requires every manufacturer, distributor, and retailer to notify the commission of any information which indicates that the product fails to comply with a product standard or has a defect. Also, notification must be made within 24 hours after the hazard is identified. If the CPSC subsequently determines that a product does, in fact, present a substantial hazard to the public, it may order the manufacturer to do one of the following:

---

[34]Any interested person may petition the Commission to issue, amend, or revoke a safety rule. The Commission must deny or grant the request within 120 days.

[35]John G. Poust and Kenneth Ross, *Products Liability of Manufacturers: Prevention and Defense*, Practicing Law Institute (New York, 1977), p. 547.

1. issue public notice of the hazard
2. issue private notice by mail to known customers and other manufacturers and distributors of the product
3. repair the defect
4. replace the product with an equivalent product
5. refund the purchase price

An imminently hazardous product is one which creates an imminent and unreasonable risk of death, serious illness, or severe personal injury. If such a product is identified, the commission may bring suit in Federal District Court to seize the product immediately. It may also require private notification to purchasers, public notification, and the recall, repair, or refund for or replacement of such product.

Requirements for New Products

The act also gives the commission authority to prescribe procedures which require manufacturers to furnish the commission with information on new consumer products before the product is distributed in commerce. A "new consumer product" is one which incorporates a design, material, or form of energy exchange which has not been used substantially in consumer products or for which there exists a lack of information adequate to assess its safety.

Penalties

Firms that violate provisions of the CPSA are subject to a $2,000 maximum civil fine for each violation and a $500,000 maximum fine for a group of related violations. Persons who receive notice of non-compliance and still knowingly and willfully violate the act are also subject to a maximum criminal penalty of $50,000 and/or not more than one year in prison.

Firms that violate commission rules are also subject to private suits when a person sustains an injury. The injured person may sue for both damages and attorney's fee.

Consumer Product Safety Commission Improvement Act

In 1976, Congress enacted the Consumer Product Safety Commission Improvement Act which permits consumers to file civil suits against the CPSC in cases of misrepresentation and negligence or when the CPSC did not exercise its powers to keep dangerous products off the market. In addition, the new law (1) allows CPSC rules to override state product safety laws in order to establish more uniformity and less confusion in regulations relative to product safety, (2) gives the CPSC authority for Federal uniform standards for the packaging of poisonous substances and for regulations covering flammable fabrics, and (3) removes pesticides, tobacco products, firearms, and ammunition from the CPSC's jurisdiction.

Product Recall

One of the most significant responses to consumer demand for product safety has been the product recall. Although product recall programs are not new,[36] the Consumer Product Safety Act of 1972 provided a formal framework for requiring firms to recall hazardous substances and an indirect mechanism for encouraging firms to recall voluntarily products known to be effective.

Formally, if the CPSC identifies that a product creates a substantial hazard, it can order the firm to recall all defective models. For example, 140,000 night-lights were recalled because they presented a severe shock hazard.[37] Informally, in order to assume a position of social responsibility and conform to governmental guidelines, some companies have taken initiative to implement programs prior to CPSC orders. For example, San Francisco Shirt Works voluntarily recalled its shirts which did not meet federal standards for flammability of clothing.[38]

As one of the most flagrant violators of product safety and warranties, the automobile industry has been singled out for special legislation to insure their conformity to product safety rules. Specifically, in 1966 Congress passed the National Traffic and Motor Vehicle Safety Act which established procedures for notifying automobile purchasers of product defects and required that the identified defects be corrected. It also gave the National Highway Traffic Safety Administration authority to recall defective automobiles and impose maximum fines of $8,000 on manufacturers that refuse to comply with recall orders.

Extended Responsibility of the CPSC

In addition to the Consumer Product Safety Act, the CPSC was given responsibility for implementing the Flammable Fabrics Act, the Federal Hazardous Substances Act, the Poison Packaging Act, and the Refrigerator Safety Act.

Flammable Fabrics Act

Congress passed the Flammable Fabrics Act as a response to the growing number of deaths and injuries caused by burning apparel. A case which

---

[36]See: *Comstock vs. General Motors,* 99 N.W. 2d 627 (Michigan, 1959). Manufacturers are compelled to warn consumers of danger.

[37]*Consumer News,* Vol. 6, No. 24 (Dec. 15, 1976), p. 2.

[38]Paul Busch, "Some Marketers Aid Product Safety Effort," *Marketing News,* Vol. 12, No. 3 (August 11, 1978), p. 4.

illustrates the pre-Flammable Fabrics Act problem involved a lady who was severely burned when her gown caught fire and instantaneously exploded into flames. The sizing of the knitted skirt of the gown, which was apparently ignited by a match or cigarette, was made of nitro-cellulose, a basic ingredient of gunpowder. After a lengthy court battle she was awarded $5,000 damages.[39]

Since the same materials that were used in the gowns and "torch" sweaters of the 1950's were legally being used in interior furnishings, baby blankets, interlining fabrics, and hand-knitted items, the law was amended in 1967 to ban all clothing, footwear, and interior furnishings that are highly flammable and, therefore, dangerous to their users.

Although not widely applied until the 1970's, the most significant aspect of the act is in developing flammability standards for fabrics. With particular emphasis on clothing, carpets, and upholstered furniture, the CPSC identifies a need, proposes a flammability standard, solicits public comment, and issues a standard. When standards are violated, the CPSC may issue cease and desist orders.

Federal Hazardous Substances Act

Hazardous substances first received attention from legislators in 1927 when they enacted the Federal Caustic Poison Act. Although the law was designed to alleviate the problem of child consumption of dangerous products, it did not keep pace with expanding technologies and the proliferation of new and dangerous products. Also, the law did not provide adequate remedies for injured consumers. When a 19-month-old child died from drinking fabric cleaner, the court indicated that the cause of death was the ingestion of the poisonous product. The manufacturer's inadequate warning only needed to reflect the product's intended use, and since drinking poison was not an intended use, the manufacturer was not liable.[40]

To reduce the probability of injury and death to children, Congress enacted the Federal Hazardous Substances Act. The Act authorized the CPSC to (1) identify substances which are hazardous to the health of consumers (including childrens' toys), (2) propose packaging and labeling requirements for substances, (3) develop standards for hazardous substances, (4) inspect manufactured products to insure conformity to standards, and (5) ban products which are hazardous or do not conform to standards. Violations of standards are subject to a maximum $500 fine and/or 90 days in prison.

[39]J. Jerome Miller, "Dressed to Kill—The Flammable Fabrics Act of 1953—Twenty Years in Retrospect," *Cumberland-Sanford Law Review,* Vol. 4 (Fall, 1973), p. 358.

[40]Craig E. Collins, "Enforcement of the Federal Hazardous Substances Act by The Consumer Product Safety Commission: Toying With the Product Safety Cycle," *Federal Bar Journal,* Vol. 34 (Spring 1975), p. 141.

Second offenses and offenses which are designed to defraud are subject to maximum $3,000 fine and/or 1 year in prison.[41]

The CPSC has also ruled that banned hazardous substances may not be sold in foreign markets.[42] Specifically, the flame-retardant chemical TRIS was found to be a potentially cancer-causing agent. Since it was used extensively on children's pajamas and other clothes, the CPSC declared that it represented a potential hazard and, therefore, banned the product as well as any products that had been treated with TRIS. Subsequent to the ban, the CPSC indicated in a policy statement that TRIS or TRIS-treated products cannot be sold in export markets, and that possible government reimbursements to companies that realized monetary losses from the ban would not apply to exporters of the product.

Poison Prevention Packaging Act

To further alleviate the problem of accidental poisoning of children, Congress passed the Poison Prevention Packaging Act. Basically, the law provided for the development of standards for packages which make accessibility to the substance difficult for small children, especially children under 5 who cannot read warning labels. Specific methods suggested for minimizing risks of ingestion include child-resistant safety caps and safety package requirements. Although primary focus of the act is on poisons which are designed for use in or around the home, it also includes poisonous products which may be stored at home but designed for use at a remote location, such as boat maintenance items and model airplane fuels.[43] In order to accommodate older people who may not be physically able to open packages which conform to specifications under the act, a special section was added which allows companies to manufacture one package size that does not meet safety closure standards.

Refrigerator Safety Act

The Refrigerator Safety Act of 1956 is also under jurisdiction of the CPSC and is designed to prevent children from becoming locked in refrigerators. The act has successfully motivated firms to conform to standards which require that refrigerators be easily openable from the inside.

---

[41]See: Franklin D. Houser, "The Consumer's Sleeping Giant, The Federal Hazardous Substances Labeling Act," *Santa Clara Lawyer*, Vol. 14 (Spring 1974), p. 535.

[42]*Prohibition of Export for TRIS-treated Garments*, "Legal Developments in Marketing," *Journal of Marketing*, Vol. 43, No. 1 (January 1979), p. 84.

[43]James J. Corrigan, "The Poison Prevention Packaging Act," *Food, Drug, Cosmetic Law Journal*, Vol. 20 (September 1971), p. 449.

Safety and the Environment—Other Laws

In addition to the Consumer Product Safety Act, Federal Hazardous Substances Act, Poison Prevention Packaging Act, and the Refrigerator Safety Act, the Toy Safety and Child Protection Act (1969) was also passed to protect children specifically. As an amendment to the Child Protection Act of 1966, the law bans the sale of hazardous toys and products intended for sale to children and requires warning labels on potentially hazardous toys.

Other acts passed to protect consumers from unhealthy products and society from hazardous substances and environmental conditions include the Safe Drinking Water Act, Clean Air Act, Solid Waste Disposal Act, Federal Water Pollution Control Act, Toxic Substances Control Act, Occupational Safety and Health Act, the Hazardous Materials Transportation Act, the Radiation Control for Health and Safety Act, the Wholesome Poultry Act, and the Wholesome Meat Act.

Packaging and Labeling

In addition to protecting products from damage in shipment and facilitating the display of products, packages have become significant sales tools for manufacturers and retailers. With the disappearance of sales people from retail stores and the proliferation of self-service shopping, the package has had to stand alone and provide consumers with sales appeal and information with which to make objective decisions. As manufacturers attempted to meet package demands created by the revolutionary development of self-service shopping, however, they somewhat ignored the information dissemination function in favor of the sales appeal objective. For example, consumer goods manufacturers would utilize packages which were significantly larger than space needed for the ingredients. One study indicated that the amount of unoccupied space in dry mix packages was 47%, the amount of space in cookie packages was 26%, and in some packages the food only occupied 20 to 25%.[44] In addition to the "slack fill" phenomenon, manufacturers would also distribute a particular brand in 40 to 50 different package sizes, use misleading illustrations of product quality, and provide insufficient identity, use, and quantity information on labels.

---

[44]Donald P. Rothschild and David W. Carroll, *Consumer Protection: Text and Materials*, 2nd Ed., Anderson Publishing Co. (Cincinnati, 1977), p. 449.

Fair Packaging and Labeling

In order to protect consumers and competitors from the deceptive packaging and labeling practices of businesses and give consumers sufficient information with which to make a decision, Congress approved passage of the Fair Packaging and Labeling Act in 1966 (FPLA).

Mandatory Label Requirements and Price Comparisons

To facilitate price comparisons and inform consumers of the product and manufacturer identity, the FPLA directed the Federal Trade Commission and the Secretary of Health, Education, and Welfare to develop mandatory rules requiring that commodity identity, manufacturer's name and address, quantity of contents, and net quantity per serving, use, or application be conspicuously displayed on the package. The Secretary was granted authority to regulate the packaging and labeling of food, drugs, cosmetics, and devices, while the FTC was given jurisdiction over packaging and labeling of other consumer commodities.

Specifically, each packaged or labeled consumer commodity must bear labels which specify the following:

(1) Specification of Identity—The common and generic product names should be conspicuously designated in easily-understood terms and located on the principal display panel.

(2) Name and Place of Business—The name and principal place of business of the manufacturer, packer, or distributor must be conspicuously identified on the product label.

(3) Net Quantity of Contents—An accurate declaration of the net quantity of contents must be conspicuously located on the label. The law delineates specifications concerning type size, location of the declaration, acceptable measuring units, and the expression of measuring units. In addition to a statement of the net quantity of contents, the label must also bear a representation of the number of servings, uses, or applications of the commodity contained in the package.

Discretionary Authority to Establish Regulations

The FPLA also gave the agencies discretionary authority to develop regulations relative to the following:

(1) Define standards for characterization of the size of a package which may be used to supplement the label statement of net quantity of contents. An example of such a standard for characterization would be "small," "medium," and "large."

(2) Regulate the placement on the package of any statement which suggests that the commodity is offered for a price lower than the customary

retail price (i.e., cents-off). The labeler cannot initiate more than 3 "cents-off" sales in the same market area for a particular size commodity during a 12-month period. At least 30 days must lapse between cents-off promotions, and a single promotion cannot last longer than 6 months during any 12 month period.

(3) Require that the common name of ingredients be listed in order of decreasing importance. The section does not require that trade secrets be divulged.

(4) Prevent the nonfunctional slack-fill of packages containing consumer commodities. Slack-filling is nonfunctional if it is done for any reason other than protection of contents or requirements of machines used for enclosing the contents in the package.

Voluntary Product Standards

If the Secretary of Commerce determines that a commodity is being distributed in an excessive number of packages of different weight or quantity, he may request that the manufacturer or distributor participate in the development of a voluntary product standard. Voluntary standards facilitate value comparisons of products by reducing the number of available package sizes.

Labeling Wool Products

In addition to the ubiquitous Fair Packaging and Labeling Act, other acts and rules have been established specifically to regulate the labeling and branding of various consumer products. The first of these statutes to be discussed is the Wool Products Labeling Act of 1939 which was designed to specify branding requirements for wool products and alleviate uncertainty which surrounded utilization of the FTC Act to attack misbranding as an unfair method of competition or a deceptive act or practice. The law was also passed to protect wool growers (i.e., sheep raisers) from the practice by manufacturers of misrepresenting the wool content of finished goods.[45] If manufacturers were allowed to misrepresent fiber content, they could sell non-wool items as wool and eventually destroy the growers' market.

The Wool Products Labeling Act required that a single stamp, tag, or label be attached to wool products and show the percentage of wool by weight and the percentage of other fibers that make up 5% or more of the product. The act also required that the name of the manufacturer of the wool product be indicated on the label. Also, imported wool products must conform to the law upon entering interstate commerce, but exported items

[45]Marshall C. Howard, "Textile and Fur Labeling Legislation: Names, Competition, and the Consumer," *California Management Review*, Vol. 14 (Winter 1971), p. 70.

need only conform to laws of the importing country. Importers of wool products, as well as textile products, may elect to use the name of the foreign manufacturer or the name, trademark, or identification number of the U.S. marketer of the products.[46] Responsibility for conforming to labeling requirements, however, rests with the company that introduces the product into interstate commerce.

Although the law has been successful in obtaining conformity to its labeling standards, the FTC still actively monitors and regulates labeling practices.[47] In one recent case, Hang Ups and Boverman Fabrics misrepresented and falsely guaranteed the woolen content of their fabrics.[48] The FTC required them to notify purchasers of the deception. In another case, four Hong Kong tailors located in Washington, D.C., falsely marketed their suits as "100 percent wool" and failed to appropriately label certain promotional samples.[49] The FTC issued a consent order for them to cease the deceptive activity.

Labeling Fur Products

Development of sophisticated dyeing and fur treating procedures was accompanied by extensive misbranding and product misrepresentation practices. Manufacturers would produce products with low-quality fur treated to appear expensive, would substitute expensive furs with cheap substitutes, and would use waste fur (i.e., tails) to construct a product which was marketed as a single fur.[50] For example, rabbit fur was represented as Arctic seal, skunk was sold as Russian sable, and Australian rabbit was treated to simulate tiger.[51]

Although the Wool Products Labeling Act is limited to misbranding activity, the Fur Products Labeling Act is designed to protect consumers against misbranding, false advertising, and false invoicing of fur products. In addition to making the distribution or sale of fur products which are misbranded, falsely advertised, or falsely invoiced an unfair method of competi-

[46]In re Steven S. Weiser, et. al., "Legal Developments in Marketing," *Journal of Marketing,* Vol. 42, No. 4 (October 1978), p. 87.

[47]In re Hang Ups Sportswear Ltd., et. al.; Boverman Fabrics, Inc., et. al., "Legal Developments in Marketing," *Journal of Marketing,* Vol. 41, No. 1 (January 1977), p. 92.

[48]*Journal of Marketing,* Vol. 41, No. 1, p. 92.

[49]Hong Kong Custom Tailors, Inc., and Affiliates, "Legal Developments in Marketing," *Journal of Marketing,* Vol. 41, No. 1 (January 1977), p. 91.

[50]Marshall C. Howard, "Textile and Fur Labeling Legislation: Names, Competition, and the Consumer," *California Management Review,* Vol. 14 (Winter 1971), p. 72.

[51]Howard, Ibid.

tion, Section 3 of the act also makes it unlawful to remove or mutilate any required label prior to sale of any fur product. It is, however, legal to substitute labels as long as the name of the person making the substitution is indicated and records which include the names of the persons from whom the fur was acquired are maintained for 3 years.

Labels on fur products must legibly indicate (1) the name or names of the animals that produced the fur, (2) whether the product is composed of used fur, (2) whether the product contains bleached or artificially-colored fur, (4) whether the fur is composed in whole or in part of paws, tails, bellies, or waste fur, (5) the names of persons who manufactured the fur, and (6) the country of origin of imported furs. The same requirements also apply to advertising or public representation of fur products. Names of furs which must be used on labels and in advertising messages were developed by the Commission with assistance from the Department of Agriculture and Department of Interior and were published in the *Fur Products Name Guide.*

Labeling Textile Fiber Products

In addition to technological advances in treating fur, there have also been significant advances in the development of man-made fibers which simulate natural fibers such as fur and cotton. Although there are major differences between the properties of synthetic and natural fibers, there are often only imperceptible differences in their appearance. Consumers could easily be persuaded to purchase an alleged fur coat when, in fact, it was simply made of synthetic fiber which simulated the actual fur in appearance and touch. In addition to problems of deception, the development and misrepresentation of these synthetics is accompanied by injury to ethical manufacturers of fur, cotton, and wool products.

In order to protect producers and consumers against misbranding and false representation of the fiber content of textile fiber products, Congress enacted the Textile Fiber Products Identification Act in 1958. Similar to the Fur Products Identification Act, the Textile Act stated that a synthetic fiber product is misbranded if it is falsely or deceptively stamped, tagged, labeled, invoiced, advertised, or otherwise identified as to the name or amount of constituent fibers contained therein. The act provided that the following must be included on the labels of textile fiber products: (1) the generic name of all natural and manufactured fiber listed in order of predominance; (2) the percentage of all fibers that make up more than 5 percent of the product; (3) name of the manufacturer; and (4) if imported, the name of the manufacturing country. If a person willfully violates the Textile Fiber Products Identification Act, the Wool Products Labeling Act, or the Fur Products

Labeling Act, the violation is declared a misdemeanor and the person is subject to a criminal penalty of $5,000 and/or 1 year imprisonment.[52]

In addition to the requirement of an identifying label, the FTC also requires that a label or tag be attached to all textile wearing apparel and piece goods which clearly discloses instructions for care and maintenance. Exempt from the 1972 Trade Regulation Rule are items that retail for less than $3.00 and are washable. Examples of appropriate care labels include "dry clean only," "hand wash cold," "do not twist or wring," "reshape," "dry flat," and "do not dry clean." Violators of the Care Labeling Rule are subject to civil penalties of $5,000 for each violation.

Labeling of Food, Drugs, and Cosmetics

Labeling of food, drugs, and cosmetics is regulated primarily by the Federal Food, Drug, and Cosmetic Act of 1938 (FFDCA), which amended the Food and Drug Act of 1906. The act gave the Food and Drug Administration (FDA) authority to control misbranding and adulteration of food, drugs, cosmetics, and therapeutic devices. These products within jurisdiction of the FDA are considered misbranded if their labels are false and misleading and are therefore likely to deceive. In addition, the FFDCA made the adulteration of food illegal. In other words, it is illegal to add any impure or inferior substances to food or omit any important ingredients. Violations of the provisions of the FFDCA may be subjected to criminal prosecution, and misbranded or adulterated products may be seized and destroyed. In addition, injunctive relief is available when the public interest is best served by removing such product from distribution or not allowing new products to be marketed.

The FDA may also develop standards of quality and identity. In order to keep manufcturers from omitting ingredients from foods, the FDA regulates and monitors the composition (i.e., quality and identity) of most consumer foods and then establishes labeling requirements which minimize the probability of deception. Relative to its "standard-setting" role, the recent direction of the FDA has been to require more informative labels. The standard for pineapple juice, for example, establishes that packers may use concentrated pineapple juice in the preparation of canned pineapple juice but must label the product as "pineapple juice from concentrate."[53] Also,

---

[52]Additional information concerning the Textile, Fur, and Wool Acts can be obtained in the following FTC publications: *Questions and Answers Relating to Textile Fiber Products Indentification Act and Regulations; Questions and Answers Relating to Fur Products Labeling Act and Regulations; Questions and Answers Relating to Wool Products Labeling Act and Regulations,* and 3 publications which delineate rules and regulations under the acts.

[53]Standards of Identity and Quality Grading for Fruit Products, "Legal Developments in Marketing," *Journal of Marketing,* Vol. 41, No. 2 (April 1977), p. 101.

instead of using general terms such as "oil" or "fats" to describe ingredients in food products, manufacturers are required to list the specific name of the oil or fat on labels.[54] The FDA has also instituted rules which require that manufacturers accurately identify the basic nature of the food. For example, if orange drink is not 100 percent orange juice, the percentage of orange juice must be listed on the label.[55] Finally, if a food resembles and is a substitute for another food, it should be designated as an imitation. If, however, the imitation is the nutritional equivalent of the other food, then the label may use a more fanciful name such as "Egg Beaters: Cholesterol-Free Egg Substitutes."[56]

Although companies are required to list ingredients in foods and drugs, the cosmetic industry avoided the regulation until the 1970's. Because of numerous reports from consumers of negative reactions to certain cosmetics, the FDA ruled that ingredients be listed on labels in order of predominance. Also, if dermatological testing proves that a particular cosmetic does not cause an adverse reaction, it may be labeled as "hypo-allergenic." The rule is designed to protect consumers by allowing comparison of ingredients in brands and avoidance of ingredients that adversely affect one's skin.[57] Cosmetic manufacturers, however, are not required to obtain FDA approval before they either manufacture and distribute a new product or add a new ingredient to an existing product. For this reason and because regulations relative to drugs are more thoroughly developed, whenever possible the FDA will attempt to establish that a questionable product is actually a drug and not a cosmetic.

The Department of Agriculture has also actively regulated labeling and quality specifications for food. In addition to controlling the labeling of meat and poultry, the department also regularly inspects food processors and maintains a quality grading program for hundreds of food products to insure that companies abide by standards. Similar to the FDA, the department develops identity and quality standards to alleviate problems associated with deceptive labeling practices. For example, in 1976 the department proposed standards to limit the amount of fat in poultry sausage products to 25 percent and to require that labels indicate whether giblets are used in the preparation of such products.[58]

[54]"Marketers Unshaken by Labeling Definition Ruling," *Advertising Age* (January 12, 1976), p. 56.

[55]Jess H. Stribling, Jr., "Regulation of Food Labeling and Advertising by the Food and Drug Administration," *Food, Drug, Cosmetic Law Journal,* Vol. 33, No. 1 (January 1978), p. 9.

[56]Stribling, p. 10.

[57]In Re Cosmetic Product Ingredient Labeling, "Legal Developments in Marketing," *Journal of Marketing,* Vol. 41, No. 4 (October 1977), p. 103.

[58]Federal Standards for Processed Meat Products, "Legal Developments in Marketing," *Journal of Marketing,* Vol. 41, No. 1 (January 1977), pp. 90-91.

Warranties

A warranty is a promise that a product is defect free and a delineation of action which will be taken in the event that the product fails to meet the seller's prior promises.[59] According to State Uniform Commercial Code (UCC), warranties may be either expressed (in writing) or implied (implication that the product is fit for a particular purpose).

Although implied warranties apply to the sale of all goods, expressed warranties are optional and are used to (1) protect buyers from product malfunctions, (2) protect sellers by limiting liability to certain aspects of the product,[60] and (3) aid the seller in promoting the product to potential buyers.

Perpetuation of Deception

In the 1950's and 1960's it became evident that the UCC was not an effective regulatory mechanism for consumer sales. Although the UCC provided merchants with guidance for development of contracts, it also gave them flexibility to adapt terms of warranty contracts to each situation. Although business may, in most cases, be familiar with the UCC and precedent setting cases that interpret the meaning of UCC articles, consumers are often ignorant of its complexities. In fact, a typical warranty contract under the UCC may be 2,000 to 3,000 words long and include extensive technical language and disclaimers which significantly limit its scope and contradict its appearance as an all-inclusive warranty. Also, responsibility for servicing products which malfunction is often not clearly delineated or assigned to a particular individual.

The complexities and ambiguities of warranties according to the UCC perpetuated deception. As stated by the Senate Committee on Commerce, "for many years warranties have confused and misled the American Consumer. A warranty is a complicated legal document whose full essence lies buried in myriads of reported legal decisions and in complicated state codes of commercial law. The consumer's understanding of what a warranty on a particular product means to him frequently does not coincide with the legal meaning."[61]

---

[59] Adapted from definition in Magnuson-Moss Warranty Act, Section 101(b).

[60] A common practice of auto manufacturers which was primarily responsible for passage of warranty legislation; see "Blame Car Makers if Tough Warranty Passes," *Advertising Age,* Vol. 42 (October 25, 1971).

[61] "Rules, Regulations, Statements and Interpretations Under Magnuson-Moss Warranty Act," *Federal Register,* Vol. 40, No. 251 (December 31, 1975).

Warranty Disclosure and Minimum Standards— New Legislation

In order to alleviate deception surrounding warranties and to provide consumers with adequate information to evaluate alternative warranties, Congress enacted the Magnuson-Moss Warranty Act. In accordance with guidelines established by the act, the FTC has established rules which require that warrantors for consumer products "fully and conspicuously disclose in simple and readily-understood language the terms and conditions of such warranty." Specifically, for consumer products costing the consumer more than $15, warrantors must disclose (1) parts or aspects of the product which are covered and not covered by the warranty, (2) remedies (including step-by-step explanation of procedures to follow) available to consumers in order to obtain performance of warranty obligations, (3) the identity of persons authorized to enforce the warranty, (4) the point in time (if other than the purchase date) when the warranty term begins, and (5) limitations on implied warranties (prominently displayed on the face of the warranty).

In addition, for consumer products which cost more than $10, warrantors must designate on their written warranties whether they are "limited" or "full." If a warranty is designated as "full," it must meet the following minimum standards:

- Warrantor must remedy defects and malfunctions within a reasonable time and without charge.
- Warrantor must not impose any limitation on the duration of any implied warranty.
- Warrantor must not exclude or limit consequential damages for breach of any written or implied warranty, unless the exclusion conspicuously appears on the face of the warranty.
- If the defect or malfunction is not remedied after a reasonable number of attempts, the consumer may elect either a full refund or replacement without charge (anti-lemon provision).

If these minimum standards are not satisfied, the warranty must be designated as "limited." Some aspects of the product may be designated as "full" and other aspects may be designated as "limited." For example, a full warranty may be extended to a refrigerator's motor while other parts are covered by a limited warranty.

Although the act does not require sellers to extend a warranty on consumer products, it does require compliance with disclosure and minimum standard rules if a warranty is given. If the warrantor fails to comply with the rules established by the FTC in accordance with the Magnuson-Moss Warranty Act, the consumer may bring suit for damages and attorney's fees. The FTC may, of course, also exercise its powers established by the FTC Act.

Trademarks

A trademark is basically a legal term which gives protection to a firm's brand name, design, and symbol. Designed to make the firm's name and image recognizable to consumers, a trademark is an important marketing tool for developing effective advertising programs, building company image, establishing customer loyalty, and differentiating one's product from competing brands.

Originally, a firm's trademark was given legal protection by the common law which prohibited competitors from using existing brand names, symbols, or designs. All a firm needed to do to preserve exclusive use of a trademark was prove that it was the first to use the mark. Because of extensive proliferation of brands and expansion of trade areas, however, common law ownership of a trademark became increasingly difficult to establish.

Trademark registration is made through the U.S. Patent and Trademark Office. After the applicant searches records to establish that the mark is not currently being used by another company, a federal application is filed. An examiner then reviews the application and determines if the mark may be registered. If application is rejected, the applicant may appeal to the Trademark Trial and Appeal Board and, subsequently, to the U.S. Court of Customs and Patent Appeals. Once the mark is approved, it must be renewed every 20 years.

In 1946, Congress enacted the Lanham Trademark Act to protect the rights of brand owners. In essence, the Lanham Act allows companies to register a brand name, symbol, or design with the U.S. Patent Office and gives the firm federal protection.

In order for the firm to receive permission to register and maintain legal rights to the trademark, however, several conditions must be satisfied. First, the firm must be able to show that it was the first to use the trademark (in the event the mark is contested by another firm). Second, the mark must be used in interstate commerce. If the firm stops using the mark, it loses all rights under the Lanham Act. Third, the mark must not be "immoral, deceptive, disparaging, a nation's insignia, likely to cause confusion with previously registered marks, merely descriptive, or merely a surname."[62] Fourth, the

---

[62]Myron L. Erickson, Thomas W. Dunke, and Frank F. Gibson, *Antitrust and Trade Regulation,* Grid, Inc. (Columbus, Ohio, 1977), p. 404.

trademark must not take on a generic characteristic. In other words, it cannot describe a general class of products.

Not only must the firm and its trademark satisfy the listed conditions prior to registration, it must continue to conform to the requirements and defend its position against challenges by other firms and governmental agencies. If, for example, the Federal Trade Commission finds that the mark has the capacity to deceive, it may excise the mark. In a case against "Dollar-A-Day" Rent-A-Car Company, the FTC and Appeals Court agreed that the rental company's name had the capacity to deceive and, therefore, should be excised.[63] The FTC can also cancel a trademark if it becomes a common, descriptive, generic name. Formica, for example, was recently challenged because it had become the common descriptive name for decorative plastic laminates used on counter tops.[64]

In addition to governmental intervention to cancel a trademark, a company may also initiate legal action to restrict the use by competitors of its trademark or of trademarks which are similar to its mark. Referred to as "trademark infringement," the primary consideration in such cases is the capacity of the copying company's mark to cause confusion among potential consumers. For example, when Helene Curtis used the brand Arm and Arm deodorant with baking soda, Church and Dwight, owner of the Arm and Hammer trademark, successfully obtained an injunction to restrict Helene Curtis from using the brand name. Not only did the similarity in name cause confusion, but Helene Curtis packaged the product with a yellow and red color combination which is distinctively identified with Arm and Hammer Baking Soda.[65] When a company such as Arm and Hammer has its rights to a trademark infringed upon, it may sue for damages, recover the offender's profits, and obtain injunctive relief against future use of the mark.

Trademark Licensing

A new and, to some groups, alarming development is government-regulated licensing of trademarks to competitors.[66] Utilizing power granted

[63]Resort Car Rental System, Inc., Brooks Rent-A-Car, Inc., Brooks Dollar-A-Day Rent-A-Car, Inc., et al. v. FTC, "Legal Developments in Marketing," *Journal of Marketing,* Vol. 40 No. 1 (January 1976), p. 93.

[64]In re FTC Petition to Trademark Trial and Appeal Board to cancel "Formica" as Trademark, "Legal Developments in Marketing," *Journal of Marketing,* Vol. 43, No. 1 (January 1979), p. 89.

[65]Church and Dwight Co., Inc. v. Helene Curtis Industries, Inc., "Legal Developments in Marketing," *Journal of Marketing,* Vol. 41, No. 4 (October 1977), p. 112; also, *Journal of Marketing,* Vol. 42, No. 2 (April 1978), p. 118.

[66]The FTC has initiated action against General Mills, General Foods, Quaker Oats, and Kellogg's for sustaining a monopolistic position through trademark promotion.

by the Federal Trade Commission Improvements Act, the FTC initiated action to require that Borden license the ReaLemon trademark to any competitor who wanted to sell reconstituted lemon juice and was willing to pay Borden a royalty of one-half of one percent of net sales.[67] The administrative law judge contended that the action was necessary because Borden had used discriminatory and predatory pricing methods to effect a monopolistic position in the processed lemon juice industry. Although the commissioners agreed with the law judge's conclusion that Borden's brand possessed monopolistic power and that Borden utilized discriminatory discounts and promotional allowances to maintain that position, they did not agree that trademark licensing was necessary to improve competition in the processed lemon juice industry. What was needed, however, was a ban on their discriminatory pricing practices.

One of the primary objectives of marketing strategy is to develop a stated image and goodwill for one's trademark. The FTC proposal penalizes companies for successfully accomplishing this objective. Although the FTC rejected use of its new remedial procedure and the courts have not reviewed its legality, the threat of future action cannot be entirely dispelled. Marketers, especially those with a dominant market position, should be aware of its implications and prepare for potential FTC challenges.

Summary

An area that has received significant attention from courts, legislatures, and consumers has been product safety. Prior to 1963, consumers could, for all practical purposes, take no action against manufacturers of defective products. In 1963, however, the Supreme Court confirmed the application of strict liability to product injury cases. In other words, after 1963, consumers had only to show that a product's defect was the cause of injury to prove that a manufacturer was liable. Although several decisions have somewhat affected manufacturer liability, significant changes in strict liability law seem to be coming from state legislatures that are enacting laws which substantially reduce manufacturer liability.

In addition to strict liability rulings of State Supreme Courts, the Federal Government has also taken an active role in protecting consumers from unsafe and defective products. Specifically, Congress enacted the Consumer Product Safety Act which established the Consumer Product Safety

---

[67]"In re Borden's ReaLemon Trademark," *Journal of Marketing,* Vol. 40, No. 4 (October 1976); also "Legal Developments in Marketing," *Journal of Marketing,* Vol. 41, No. 1 (January 1977), p. 98.

Commission (CPSC). The CPSC's functions are to (1) identify, monitor, and ban hazardous products, (2) develop quality control standards for products and (3) develop programs to alleviate injuries and educate consumers. In addition, the Consumer Product Safety Commission Improvement Act amended the original law to give the Commission more jurisdiction and power as well as to give consumers the right to sue the CPSC if it does not properly perform its function.

Regulation of packaging and labeling came primarily from the Fair Packaging and Labeling Act. The Law requires that labels specifically identify the product's identity, the name and address of the manufacturer, and net quantity of contents. The law also requires the listing of ingredients and defines standards for package size characterization (i.e., small, medium, large). Labeling requirements for specific products were established with enactment of the Wool Products Labeling Act, Fur Products Labeling Act, Textile Fiber Products Identification Act, and Food, Drug and Cosmetic Act.

Because of the inadequacy of the UCC to protect consumers from deceptive warranty practices of manufacturers, Congress enacted the Magnuson-Moss Warranty Act. In essence, the warranty act required that warrantors "fully and conspicuously disclose in simple and readily understood language the terms and conditions of such warranty." It also established strict compliance requirements for warranties that were designated as "full."

Discussion Questions

1. Evaluate the provisions of the Magnuson-Moss Warranty Act. Do the provisions effectively alleviate warranty problems of the 1950's and 1960's?

2. What organizational and administrative steps should be taken to alleviate problems associated with product recall?

3. What are the consequences to society of a system of strict liability? Also, what can be done to alleviate these problems of strict liability?

4. One purpose of the Fair Packaging and Labeling Act was to facilitate price comparisons. Do you feel that the Act accomplishes that objective?

5. Cite companies that have taken an obvious interest in the safety of consumers. What have these companies done to perpetuate safety in products?

6. Are manufacturers liable for injuries which result from consumer misuse of a product? Should they be liable?

7. Should Government agencies or courts be allowed to restrict the use of ones own brand name because they feel that it has become a generic term?

7 CONSUMER RIGHT TO KNOW

Up to this point, this book has focused on the various areas of marketing management and the legal statutes and precedents that significantly affect the marketer's flexibility to formulate appropriate strategies. As evidenced by prior chapters, the government's regulatory efforts have pervaded all aspects of the marketing mix—pricing, distribution, promotion, and product development. Although many of the regulations were designed to either protect the free enterprise system by stimulating competition or protect consumers from dangerous and defective products and product designs, several additional laws were formulated simply to inform consumers that they might be better, more competent purchasers. These statutes which require businesses to provide their customers with certain information reflect the recent "consumer right to know" mandate of the 1960's and 70's.

Although "consumer right to know" is not a new concept, most laws prior to the 1960's were negative—they indicated what could not be done (i.e., deceive consumers) but not what must be done to inform consumers. The only laws prior to the 1960's that affirmatively outlined what must be done to inform consumers were directed specifically at several industries in which widespread consumer abuse was recognized. The fur, textile, and wool labeling laws (Chapter 6) were developed to stop the fraudulent practices of misrepresenting actual materials used in the manufacture of various garments. Also, the Automobile Disclosure Act of 1958, which required dealers to display the manufacturer's suggested retail price on all new cars, was an initial attempt to alleviate deception in an industry that, according to many observers, vitally needed reforming.

The proliferation of brand alternatives and the pervasive development of self-service shopping created problems which could not adequately be resolved by pre-1966 consumer legislation. For some products, there would be several dozen brand alternatives contained in 40 or 50 different package

141

sizes. Value comparison of this enormous number of alternatives was, for all practical purposes, impossible. In addition to problems associated with value comparison, identification and comparison of product characteristics were also difficult. Since sales clerks had been replaced with the self-service institution, responsibility for identifying and evaluating the physical aspects of products was delegated to consumers. The inadequacy of information on packages made this task almost as insurmountable as comparing relative value.

Once the difficult task of brand selection had been accomplished, the consumer was then confronted with the problem of actually making a purchase. For consumers who made cash purchases, no significant problems were realized, but for those who preferred open-ended credit transactions, their problems were in many cases only beginning. Since the law did not require the meaningful disclosure of credit terms, even the most sophisticated shopper generally agreed to abstruse credit terms. Also, if a mistake were made on a customer's bill, the customer was usually unfamiliar with formal procedures for resolving the dispute. Under the law, the creditor was not obligated to facilitate the dispute settlement procedure.

Thus, numerous brand alternatives, self-service shopping, and credit buying opened a new field of proposed legislation designed to resolve consumer problems and reflect the Government's "consumer right to know" mandate. Today, new laws aid the buyer in matters of lending, collections, discrimination, pricing, and packaging—topics which are discussed in this chapter.

Credit

Consumers' use of credit to purchase everything from homes to groceries has become an accepted and, to many, a preferred way of obtaining consumer goods and services. Consistent with the convenience-orientation of the twentieth century consumer, utilization of credit expanded rapidly during the 1960's and 1970's. Consumers can now use the telephone to shop from catalogs, commercials, direct mail ads, and other product information sources. They can also enjoy immediate product benefits by deferring payment rather than delaying purchases until the amount is saved.

Appearing concurrently with the need for consumer credit were institutions that attempted to fulfill that need. Many of these institutions envisioned the rapidly-expanding market for credit as an opportunity to realize excessive profits at the expense of the unwary consumer. Credit charge calculations and contracts were complex, and most consumers did not have adequate training to evaluate actual credit charges and interpret "fine print" disclaimers.

Truth in Lending

To alleviate the problem of deceptive credit practices among lending institutions and to reinforce its "consumer right to know" mandate, Congress enacted the Consumer Credit Protection Act in 1968. Title I of the new statute, known as the Truth in Lending Act, was designed to "assure a more meaningful disclosure of credit terms" so that the consumer could intelligently compare alternative credit plans and make informed decisions. The act also directed the Board of Governors of the Federal Reserve Board to prescribe rules to facilitate implementation and satisfaction of the act's purpose. The board satisfied its directive by promulgating Regulation Z. Although the act required that creditors conspicuously disclose to individual customers the cost of obtaining credit by expressing the dollar amount of finance charges and the annual percentage rate, it did not control the amount of interest charge to customers.

In order to accomplish the information disclosure objectives of Truth in Lending, the act and Regulation Z prescribe the following rules:

• Finance charge must include all direct and indirect charges that are incident to or a condition of the extension of credit. Charges that are within the scope of this requirement and, therefore, must be included in the finance charge encompass interest, service charges, loan fee, finder's fee, fee for credit reports or investigations, and fee for insurance that is connected with the loan. Some charges, however, such as taxes, certificate of title fee, and registration fees may be excluded from the finance charge but must be itemized and disclosed to the customer.

• For open-end credit accounts such as credit cards, the annual percentage rates must be computed "so as to permit disclosure with an accuracy at least to the nearest quarter of 1 percent." For both open-ended credit accounts and accounts other than open-ended, Regulation Z specifically states methods and guidelines for calculating and presenting these charges to the customer.

• Finance charges or, for open-ended accounts, conditions and computing methods under which finance charges will be assessed must be clearly and conspicuously disclosed to customers prior to making a transaction or opening an account.

• Customers who use their home as collateral for a loan may cancel the transaction until midnight of the third business day after consummation of the transaction.

• Credit card holders are liable for unauthorized use of their cards up to $50 if the issuer gives notice of the potential liabilities and provides a self-addressed, prestamped notification to be mailed in the event of loss or theft.

Truth in lending, as supplemented by Regulation Z, extensively specifies how to conform to rules of disclosure, how to calculate finance charges, and how to resolve errors. Violators of the consumer's right to know, as specified in the Truth in Lending Act, are subject to civil liability of two times the finance charge in connection with the transaction. The violator must also pay court costs and reasonable attorney's fees. Willful and knowing violation of the statute is a criminal offense, and the violator is subject to a $5,000 maximum fine and imprisonment for a maximum of 1 year. Violators are subject to penalty from the Federal Trade Commission.

In addition, the scope of the act also extends to advertising credit terms. Specifically, creditors can make statements about downpayments, installment plans, and amount of credit only if the advertised arrangements are normally or customarily made by the creditor. Also, a creditor cannot advertise a specific credit term unless all other terms are stated clearly in the advertisement.

Finally, exempted from the provisions of Truth in Lending are (1) business or governmental credit transactions, (2) transactions on security or commercial accounts, (3) non-real property credit over $25,000, (4) transactions under public utility tariffs, (5) agricultural credit transactions with over $25,000 financed, and (6) lease transactions of personal property which provide that "the lease has no liability for the value of the property at the end of the lease term except for abnormal wear and tear and the lessee has no option to purchase the leased property."

Fair Credit Billing Act

As an amendment to the Truth in Lending Act, the Fair Credit Billing Act of 1975 is designed to help consumers correct mistakes made on billing statements of their open-ended credit plans. The Act requires creditors to provide customers with a copy of its dispute settlement procedure every six months or summarize the procedure on each monthly statement.[1] The procedure must inform the customer how to notify the creditor of billing errors, what the creditor must do in the event of an error, how the customer is protected from collection and bad debt reports, what happens when a dispute is or is not settled, how the creditor can be penalized if the procedure is not followed, and when the customer can withhold payment for purchases made on a credit card. If the billing correction procedure is not followed, the creditor cannot collect the first $50 of the disputed charge, even if the bill was correct. Also, consumers may sue for damages and attorney's fees which result from the creditor's failure to comply with the act.

In addition to informing customers of bill correction procedures, Fair

[1]Copies of the detailed procedure must be made available to customers upon request.

Credit Billing also allows creditors to give discounts for cash purchases, requires creditors to credit a customer's account promptly for returned merchandise and refund any overpayments if requested by the customer, and requires creditors to mail a statement of account for each billing period.

Fair Credit Reporting Act

The Fair Credit Reporting Act was passed in 1971 to amend the Consumer Credit Protection Act. It protects consumers against the dissemination of inaccurate information which may restrict the chances of obtaining credit, insurance, or employment. Credit bureaus are frequently asked to provide information on the credit history of potential employees or customers. If a credit report contains negative information, it may restrict the consumer's ability to obtain credit. Prior to passage of the Fair Credit Reporting Act (FCRA), consumers were seldom given access to reports and were denied the opportunity to correct inaccurate information. To protect consumers against such inequities, FCRA requires credit agencies to exercise fairness and impartiality in fulfilling their responsibilities and places consumer disclosure responsibilities on users of credit reports.

The most significant aspect of FCRA is to give consumers the right to know why adverse action is taken with respect to a consumer application. Specifically, if a consumer's application for credit, employment, or insurance is rejected, the user of such a report must inform the consumer of the name and address of the consumer reporting agency. The consumer can then obtain, free of charge from the reporting agency, the nature, substance, and sources of the information. If credit was not previously denied, the consumer may, for a reasonable fee, still obtain any information that reflects his credit worthiness, credit standing, credit capacity, character, general reputation, personal characteristics, or mode of living. He also has the right to identify who received reports during the preceding six months for credit or insurance purposes and during the preceding two years for employment purposes.[2] If a consumer disputes a reported item, the agency must reinvestigate and delete any inaccurate or unverifiable information from the report. If the dispute is not resolved, a statement of the consumer's position must be included in the file and must be sent to certain businesses without charge if such a request is made within 30 days of an adverse action.

Adverse information may be maintained in the agency's files for only 7 years, and bankruptcy information may be reported for only 14 years. If this provision or any additional provision is willfully violated, the consumer may seek actual damages sustained as a result of noncompliance, punitive

[2]Note that information can only be reported for legitimate business purposes.

damages, court costs, and reasonable attorney's fees. For negligent non-compliance, the consumer may obtain actual damages, court costs, and attorney's fees. Obtaining information from a consumer reporting agency under false pretenses is punishable by a $5,000 fine and a maximum of one year imprisonment.

The act also covers disclosure of investigative reports which are based on interviews with friends, neighbors, and other persons. Specifically, agencies which investigate or commission to have investigated a person's character, general reputation, personal characteristics, and mode of living must (1) disclose their intentions to conduct the investigation not later than 3 days after a request for the report was made and (2) inform the consumer of his right to obtain a disclosure of the nature and scope of the investigation.

Credit Discrimination and Illegal Collection

In addition to credit disclosure laws that reflect the consumer right to know mandate, there are several credit laws that affect marketing. First, the Equal Credit Opportunity Act of 1975, as supplemented by Regulation B in 1977, prohibits discrimination in any aspect of a credit transaction because of sex, marital status, race, national origin, religion, age, or receipt of public financial assistance (i.e., social security). This means that the creditor may not ask an applicant questions pertaining to personal characteristics listed in the preceding sentence. Creditors also may not ask questions about the applicant's spouse unless the account will be used by the spouse, the applicant relies on the spouse's income, or the applicant lives in a community property state.

The Equal Credit Opportunity Act is designed to make evaluation of credit worthiness more objective by requiring creditors to consider such factors as income, debts, and past credit history. It restricts them from categorizing certain consumers, such as women, as bad risks and summarily denying them credit. It also helps married women by allowing them to get credit in their own name or married name, obtain credit without a co-signer, and have their family credit history recorded in both their name as well as their husband's name.

Creditors are required to give applicants notice of acceptance or rejection within 30 days of the filing date. Specific reasons must be given for a rejected application. As indicated in a complaint filed against Montgomery Ward, simply advising applicants that their total score under a credit scoring system is not high enough does not satisfy the requirement that the creditor give specific reasons for rejection.[3] Reasons such as the following must be given: "Your income is not high enough."

[3]In re Montgomery Ward and Co., Inc., "Legal Developments in Marketing," *Journal of Marketing,* Vol. 41, No. 3 (July 1977), p. 115.

Finally, violators of the Equal Credit Opportunity Act may be sued for actual damages, a maximum of $10,000 in punitive damages, court costs, and attorney's fees. Also, if other people are also damaged by discriminatory credit practices of one company, they may unite and bring a class action suit against the company for punitive damages of up to $500,000 or 1 percent of the company's net worth, whichever is less.

Another unscrupulous credit practice of business is the utilization of scare tactics to collect installment payments. Walter-Thomas Furniture Company, for example, allegedly called customers early in the day and late at night, contacted employers to embarrass customers into paying, used intimidation and threats to repossess products without due process of law, and took items when customers were not at home.[4] Although deceptive credit practices could successfully be attacked as unfair acts, a law was passed in 1978 to deal specifically with this growing problem. The new law, known as the Fair Debt Collection Practices Act, makes it illegal for a debt collector to harass or abuse any person and make false statements or use unfair methods when collecting a debt.[5] Although the law does not cancel a debtor's obligation to pay, it does give the debtor the right to sue violators for damages, court costs, and attorney's fees.

Price and Package Disclosure

As was indicated in Chapter 6, packaging and labeling disclosure requirements were enacted to facilitate consumer decision-making and prevent deception. Fair Packaging and Labeling Acts, the Federal Trade Commission Act, the Federal Food Drug, and Cosmetic Act, the wool, textile, and fur labeling laws, the Magnuson-Moss Warranty Act, and the Automobile Information Disclosure Act of 1958 all enable the consumer to understand and ascertain more readily the quality and price of the goods he is buying.

Although package, label, and advertising laws have been successful at reducing deception by requiring accurate disclosure of information, they have not significantly reduced the burdensome and overwhelming task of comparing alternative values. The large number of brands and package sizes makes evaluation of value a time-consuming and difficult task. When buying canned beans, for example, consumers may have to choose between 10

---

[4]In re Walter-Thomas Furniture Company, "Legal Developments in Marketing," *Journal of Marketing,* Vol. 40, No. 3 (July 1976), p. 96.

[5]Fair Debt Collection Practices Act, "Legal Developments in Marketing," *Journal of Marketing,* Vol. 42, No. 4 (October 1978), p. 87.

different brands and 3 package sizes for each brand. To determine the best buy, consumers are required to divide the price of each brand by the number of ounces in the various packages. To complicate comparison shopping even more, there is not necessarily a relationship between package size and value. A large can of green beans, therefore, may be more expensive per ounce than a small can of beans.

Unit Pricing

To alleviate value comparison problems at retail, legislators and consumer groups have suggested that retailers display a shelf tag for each brand and package size which expresses price in some standard unit of measure. The price of canned beans, for example, would be expressed as a price per ounce. The price of other products may be identified as price per pound, price per pint, etc. The primary benefit of such pricing, therefore, is a common denominator which can be used by consumers to identify the lowest priced item.

Although no federal law presently requires retailers to make unit prices available to consumers, the Government has been considering a bill, the Price Disclosure Act, which would require unit pricing of packaged consumer goods. Such laws have already been passed in local municipalities but have been held up in Congress until more insight can be gained into the influence of unit prices on consumer decision behavior. Also, Congress seems to be waiting to determine if retailers will voluntarily continue to implement unit pricing policies which have already become widespread throughout the nation.

Ultimately, continued utilization of unit pricing systems will be determined by examining and balancing costs and competitive advantages realized from implementing and maintaining such systems. Costs of installation and maintenance costs may be as high as $1,500 and $750 per store, respectively.[6] Also, consumer acceptance of unit pricing systems has been somewhat favorable; some studies indicate that at least 30 percent of consumers regularly rely on such prices for product value comparison.[7] This phenomenon is especially widespread among higher-educated consumers.

Mandatory Pricing

Mandatory pricing requires retailers of packaged consumer goods to indicate the price of all consumer goods on the product or package rather

[6]Albert D. Bates, *Retailing and Its Environment,* D. Van Nostrand Company (New York, 1979), p. 198.

[7]Joseph C. Seibert, *Concepts of Marketing Management,* Harper and Row (New York, 1973), p. 457.

than on the shelf. Although such a requirement has been initiated in several states and cities, there are no laws that require compliance to mandatory pricing on a national level. The Price Disclosure Act, however, an amendment to the Fair Packaging and Labeling Act aimed at unit pricing, would require national compliance.

Moves to eliminate individually-priced items have come from retail grocery chains that prefer to use shelf pricing in order to accommodate the use of electronic scanning systems. With the scanning device, the product is passed over the scanner's light beam, which reads a 10-digit universal product code and alerts the computer to find the corresponding price. Subsequently, the computer indicates the price on an electronic screen as well as on a receipt which details the price, store location, item description, date and time of transaction, checkout lane, product weight, and other pricing data.

The reason retailers prefer to avoid mandatory pricing when using scanners is that the price in the computer is easily updated whenever price changes occur, while prices on inventory remain until the items are sold. Retailers, therefore, fear that prices in the computer will oftentimes correspond inaccurately to prices on individually-marked items. Shelf prices, however, could easily be changed to reflect updated prices in the computer.

Although many of the problems surrounding mandatory pricing may be solved with new technology, decisions relative to marketing law can be difficult in light of the initial advantages and disadvantages of the public policy issue. For example, consider the advantages of automatic scanners. First, since scanners are approximately 20 percent faster than manual checkout methods, retailers provide better service during high traffic periods, utilize fewer checkout stations, reduce labor costs, and therefore realize lower prices to consumers. Second, consumers and retailers benefit from the elimination of under- and over-charges. Third, optional scanning frees the cashier to improve his customer relation role. Finally, the detailed tape may be maintained and used by consumers to compare prices over a time period and between stores. However, these advantages could disappear with passage of a federal Price Disclosure Act.

Although certain benefits are realized from employing optical scanners, there are also certain disadvantages which complicate public policy decision-making. First, utilization of UPC codes and shelf prices gives retailers the opportunity to overprice merchandise fraudulently. In other words, a shelf price could indicate a merchandise value of 29¢ while the actual price, which is stored in the computer, could be 38¢. Of course, the scanner records a price of 38¢ and the consumer is overcharged 9¢. Second, there is no assurance that price tags will be on the shelves. In fact, a recent study by Michigan State University indicated that 12 percent of the consumers in stores not using item pricing could not find product price on the shelf. In conventional stores that had each item individually marked, only 4 percent were unable to identify the price.[8] Third, some customers like to check the accuracy of the store by comparing the price on the package with the corresponding price on the register tape. Since no price appears on the product, it is impossible to make these comparisons unless the consumer remembers shelf prices or writes them down while shopping.

Open Dating

Open dating involves placing a date on perishable and semiperishable foods which represents the last day the food should be maintained on a grocer's shelf. By selling the item on or before the suggested date, the product will theoretically not spoil before the product can reasonably be expected to be consumed.

As reported by Nayak and Rosenberg, most consumers are generally satisfied with the freshness of food in grocery stores. Most manufacturers agree with this observation and state that improvements in food packaging, storing, and processing have lengthened the shelf life of food and alleviated the need for open dating. Although consumers like open dating and are possibly more confident of the "dated" product's freshness, they are unwilling to assume the higher costs that are associated with the implementation of this consumer right to know policy.[9]

Similar to mandatory pricing and unit pricing, open dating does little more than provide consumers with additional and, in most cases, unneeded information. While credit, packaging, warranty, labeling, and product disclosures have attacked deception and have significantly aided decision-making, the pricing and dating programs simply expand awareness and, to a small degree, facilitate decision-making. For these reasons the government has been reluctant to mandate open dating as a worthy addition to the existing consumer right to know legislation.

Although open dating requirements have been established in some municipalities, information gathered from conversations with FTC personnel indicates that the government favors voluntary program development over mandatory statutory requirements. In fact, there is some indication that the Price Disclosure Act to require unit and mandatory pricing was proposed primarily to coerce grocers into voluntary compliance.

[8]John Allen, Gilbert Harrell, and Michael Hutt, *Consumer Shopping Behavior Pricing Study,* for the Public Policy Subcommittee of the Ad Hoc Committee on the Universal Product Code, National Association of Food Chains, Washington, D. C., 1976.

[9]Prabhaker Nayak and Larry J. Rosenberg, "Does Open Dating of Food Products Benefit the Consumer?" *Journal of Retailing,* Vol. 51, No. 2 (Summer 1975), pp. 10-20.

Summary and Evaluation

In summary, consumers have been given the right to know. They have demanded and received the right to examine governmental activity by the Freedom of Information Act. Informative disclosure of product ingredients and characteristics has been facilitated by the various labeling laws. Effective product selection decisions through objective analysis of variables at retail was promoted with Fair Packaging and Labeling. Provisions for additional decision-making data such as unit prices, mandatory prices, and open dates are being contemplated at state, local, and federal levels. Credit disclosure and the attendant "right to know" provisions were accomplished by Truth in Lending, Fair Credit Reporting, and Fair Credit Billing. Finally, truth in advertising has come closer to becoming a reality through affirmative disclosure requirements, advertising substantiation guidelines, and the corrective advertising remedy.

Such legislation has benefited consumers. In the future, though, new questions must be asked about consumer laws. What objectives are served by the law? Are these objectives accomplished with existing legislation? Are there alternative methods of accomplishing the same objectives? How much are consumers willing to pay for additional information? Implementation of disclosure requirements is expensive to both business and the consumer, and such questions must be examined before new programs receive government sanction. Since information disclosure requirements are relatively new, little is known about the impact on consumers and business. Although some research has suggested that information disclosure increases confidence in business and products,[10] there is insufficient evidence to identify specifically whether consumers use available information or how it will be used. This lack of research supports one of the primary criticisms of consumer right to know efforts: government takes an action without adequate understanding of its implications. Only the coming years will be able to answer whether or not such actions merited sanction.

Discussion Questions

1. What questions should be answered by Congress before "consumer right to know" legislation is enacted?

---

[10]George S. Day, "Assessing the Effects of Information Disclosure Requirements," *Journal of Marketing,* Vol. 40, No. 2 (April 1976), p. 45.

2. The purpose of the consumer protection/right to know movement is to make consumers more informed, efficient shoppers. In addition to the enactment of laws to accomplish this objective, what additional alternatives are available?

3. What future direction do you believe the Government should take relative to its "consumer right to know" mandate?

4. What problem do you think the Government will have in accomplishing objectives of existing "consumer right to know" legislation?

CASE INDEX

153

SUBJECT INDEX